GRENADA
WHOSE FREEDOM?

Latin America Bureau

Special Brief

First published in Great Britain in 1984 by

Latin America Bureau (Research and Action) Ltd
1 Amwell Street
London EC1R 1UL

ISBN 0 906156 25 4

Written by Fitzroy Ambursley and James Dunkerley
Additional Material by Winston James, Jenny Pearce, Hugh
O'Shaughnessy, Jonathan Bloch, Pat Fitzgerald and Dorothy
Wade
Design by Jan Brown Designs
Maps by Michael Green
Photographs by Jenny Matthews
Typeset, printed and bound by Russell Press Ltd., Nottingham
Trade Distribution by Third World Publications

Contents

Foreword

The invasion of Grenada by US forces on 25 October 1983 was a major international incident producing extensive comment in the world's press and concentrating attention on a tiny island that many people had scarcely heard of. Four months after the event Grenada had gone out of the news; Washington appeared to have succeeded in its calculated risk of breaking international law, and an apparent calm had settled over the Caribbean. One reason for the short-term success of the US operation undoubtedly lay in the prior collapse of the People's Revolutionary Government of Grenada and the assassination of its leader, Maurice Bishop. This remarkable event not only provided Washington with a spurious rationale for its violation of Grenada's sovereignty but also gravely disorientated those people who were in the best position to oppose and denounce it.

Although several detailed studies of the invasion and the rule of the New Jewel Movement (NJM) are now in preparation, we believe that there is a need for a brief informative survey of the events of October 1983 and their background. Writing so soon after the event and with limited space it has been possible only to touch on major developments and the principal issues at stake. We have not discussed at length many of the features of the NJM's 'peaceful revolution' — the 'revo' as it was known to many Grenadians — which made it both extremely popular and also very vulnerable. If anything, we have emphasised the problems of the period 1979 to 1983, but it should be stressed that those years were unique in Grenadian history and will be remembered with deep affection by most of the island's population as having given them a sense of identity, a better standard of living and unprecedented freedom.

This Special Brief does not deal with US policy towards Grenada and the Caribbean in great detail since this has already been surveyed in our publication *Under the Eagle*, which places the events discussed here in a wider context. In the future we plan to publish a study of the banana industry in the Eastern Caribbean and a critique of development models in the region. These studies will develop discussion of some of the issues mentioned in the present essay.

Two members of the Latin America Bureau were in Grenada during the week of invasion and talked to many people, including members of the invasion forces and supporters of both Maurice Bishop and Bernard Coard within the NJM. These discussions have persuaded us that the internal documents of the party referred to and partially reprinted here are authentic and a valuable source of information. We believe that the developments inside the NJM over September and October 1983 were of such importance that reference to these sources is essential. At the same time, the analysis presented here is the result of a collaborative appraisal of the crisis of the Grenadian revolution; none of the individuals contributing to this publication is in complete agreement with every statement made here. However, we do consider that this small book is a valid contribution to the debate over what happened in Grenada. It has been written in the hope that in the aftermath of the invasion people will not forget that country, ignore the achievements of its short-lived revolution, or acquiesce in Washington's continued domination, which impedes progress towards the establishment of more just, equitable and peaceful societies in Grenada and the rest of the Caribbean and Central America.

James Dunkerley
Latin America Bureau
February 1984

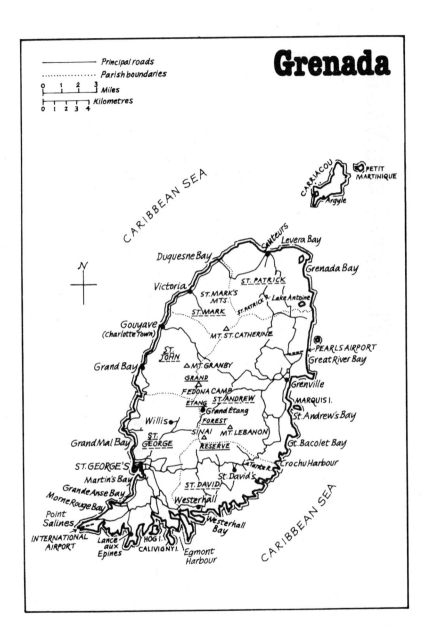

Grenada

Principal roads
Parish boundaries

Miles 0 1 2 3
Kilometres 0 1 2 3 4

CARIBBEAN SEA

CARRIACOU

PETIT MARTINIQUE

Argyle

Couteurs

Levera Bay

Duquesne Bay

Grenada Bay

Victoria

ST. PATRICK

ST. MARK'S MTS.

ST. PATRICK

Lake Antoine

Gouyave (Charlotte Town)

ST. MARK

MT. ST. CATHERINE

PEARLS AIRPORT

ST. JOHN

Great River Bay

Grand Bay

MT. GRANBY

GRAND

FEDONA CAMP

Grenville

ETANG

ST. ANDREW

MARQUIS I.

Grand Étang

St. Andrew's Bay

Willis

FOREST

SINAI

MT. LEBANON

ST. GEORGE

RESERVE

Gt. Bacolet Bay

Grand Mal Bay

La Tante R.

Crochu Harbour

ST. GEORGE'S

Martin's Bay

St. David's

Grande Anse Bay

ST. DAVID

Morne Rouge Bay

Westerhall

Point Salines

Westerhall Bay

INTERNATIONAL AIRPORT

Lance aux Epines

HOG I.

CALIVIGNY I.

Egmont Harbour

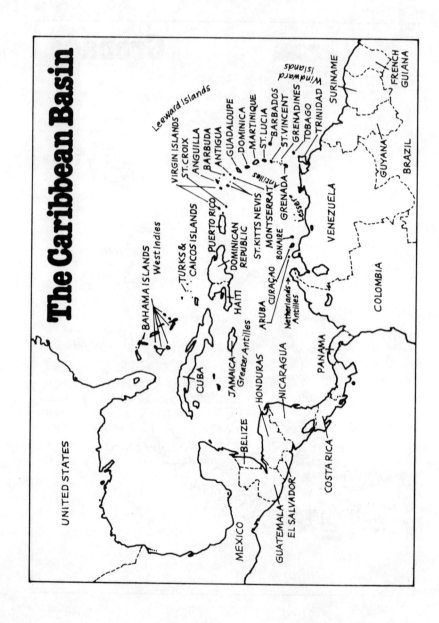

The Caribbean Basin

1 Grenada in Brief

Statistics

Area	344 sq km (75,370 acres)
Population	Total 110,000 (1980)
	Natural Growth 1.9% (1970)
	Net Migration − 6.0% (1970-79)
Principal Town	St George's (8,000)

The People

Origins	African 80%; East Indian 3%; Mixed 10% (1970)
Language	English; local patois
Religion	Roman Catholic 60%; Anglican 20%; Methodist 3%; Seventh Day Adventist 3%; other Protestant denominations 4.5%

The Economy   GDP Per Capita US$625 (1980)

Exports	1979 US$21.7 million
	1980 US$17.0 million
	1981 US$18.8 million
	1982 US$18.5 million
Imports	1979 US$53.6 million
	1980 US$52.2 million
	1981 US$58.0 million
	1982 US$60.7 million
Principal Exports	Cocoa 44%; nutmeg 28%; bananas 21%; mace 3% (In 1978 tourism accounted for 4% of GDP)

Major Trading Partners	Exports to UK 43.9%; Canada 3.2%; USA 3.1%; Caricom 9.0%; Imports from UK 17.9%; Canada 5.7%; USA 19.4%; Caricom 37.4%
Aid (1979-82)	Cuba 67.6%; Arab world 15.5%; Multilateral organisations (EEC; OAS; UNICEF etc.) 11.5%; USSR 2.2%; UK 0.7%
Foreign Debt	1978 US$7.5m (12.1% GDP; 2.7% exports); 1981 US$17.1m (17.7% GDP; 3.7% exports)
Unemployment	1979 49%; 1982 14.3%.
Literacy	1979 80% 1982 95%
Health	Life expectancy at birth 69 years (1979); Infant mortality per thousand live births 27.6 (1976); Doctors per head 1979 one per 4,000; 1982 one per 3,000
Education	Secondary schooling for those eligible: 1978 11%; 1982 36%

Sources: Central Statistics Office, *Grenada: Abstract of Statistics 1979;* World Bank, *Economic Memorandum on Grenada,* August 1982; Bernard Coard, *Report on the National Economy for 1981;* Instituto de Investigaciones Economicas y Sociales, Nicaragua, *Pensamiento Propio.*

Chronology

1950   Eric Gairy founds the Grenada Mental and Manual Workers Union (GMMWU).

1951   Gairy rises to prominence as a strike leader and wins the general election.

1962   Gairy's government is dismissed for corruption and the constitution is suspended; the Grenada National Party (GNP) wins subsequent election.

1967   Grenada becomes an Associated State with Britain handling its external affairs; Gairy wins election.

1972   Gairy wins election.
March — Joint Endeavour for the Welfare, Education and Liberation of the People (JEWEL) formed by teachers and rural workers.
September — Movement for Assemblies of the People (MAP) emerges in St George's.

1973   Upsurge of popular unrest as Gairy's secret police become more brutal and democratic liberties are extensively repressed.
March — JEWEL and MAP form the New Jewel Movement (NJM).
November — Leaders of the NJM are viciously assaulted while planning a general strike.

1974   January — General strike called; police repression during three month stoppage includes assassination of Rupert Bishop, father of NJM leader Maurice.
February 7 — Grenada becomes independent in the dark; the strike continues. NJM leadership arrested before the ceremony.

1976   The People's Alliance, including the NJM, GNP and United People's Party (UPP) greatly reduces Gairy's majority in a poll of questionable honesty.

1979   March 13 — NJM militants storm the True Blue barracks and oust Gairy in a coup that costs only three lives. Bishop becomes prime minister in the People's Revolutionary Government (PRG) and applies to both capitalist and socialist countries for aid; after a month only Cuba and Guyana have responded. Health care and free education established; Britain cuts aid.

1980   Establishment of fish processing plant; agrarian reform begins with 'idle lands for idle hands' campaign.
June — Bomb explosion at St George's rally attended by PRG leaders and Cuban ambassador; three young women are killed.

1981   August 19-21 — US-led NATO exercise 'Ocean Venture 81' takes place in the Caribbean. CIA covert operations plan against Grenada rejected by US Senate Intelligence Committee. Bishop appeals for guarantees to the UN.

1982   IMF congratulates PRG for economic performance.

July — Bishop visits Moscow and obtains long-term credits.

August — Jamaica and Barbados attempt to oust Grenada from the Caribbean Economic Community (Caricom).

October — Bernard Coard resigns from the NJM Central Committee.

November — US 'Ocean Venture' manoeuvres prompt increased preparation of popular militia against a possible invasion.

1983   March 23 — Reagan claims in a major speech that Grenada is a threat to US security and that the airport under construction at Point Salines is to be a Soviet military base. US naval manoeuvres under way in the Caribbean.

March 25 — Bishop denies US claims, warns against invasion, and puts People's Revolutionary Army (PRA) and militia on full alert.

June — Maurice Bishop and PRG delegation visit US in an effort to improve relations. Reagan refuses to receive them.

September — Gairy holds meetings with exiles from the Grenadian Democratic Movement (GDM) in Barbados.

September 14-16 — NJM central committee discusses party problems and proposal for joint leadership between Bishop and Coard.

September 25 — NJM membership approves joint leadership.

September 28 — Bishop, Foreign Minister Unison Whiteman and others leave on visit to eastern Europe.

October 8 — Delegation returns after brief stay in Cuba.

October 12 — Widespread rumours that Coard and his wife Phyllis are plotting to kill Bishop; Bishop accused of spreading these rumours and deprived of security staff by the central committee.

October 13 — Bishop placed under house arrest but continues to hold the office of prime minister. NJM membership votes in support of the measure.

October 14 — Radio Free Grenada (RFG) announces that Coard has replaced Bishop; later this statement is retracted. Coard announces his resignation as deputy prime minister.

October 15 — Tom Adams, premier of Barbados, is approached by a US official who suggests that Bishop be rescued. Negotiations between Coard and Bishop's supporters start. Kenrick Radix arrested after pro-Bishop demonstration.

October 16 — Journalists ordered off the island. PRA

commander General Hudson Austin accuses Bishop of 'onemanism' and spreading rumours about Coard.

October 17 — Unison Whiteman flies back from UN.

October 18 — Fitzroy Bain, George Louison, Unison Whiteman and Lyden Ramdhanny resign from PRG; Louison is arrested. Hundreds of schoolchildren occupy Pearls airport chanting 'No Bishop, no school'. Widespread popular discontent over Bishop's detention.

October 19 — 9.30-10.30am Whiteman leads a crowd of several thousand to Bishop's house and releases him and Jacqueline Creft.

11.00am — Crowd marches to Fort Rupert, where there is no real resistance from military personnel. The crowd waits outside while Bishop and some 30 supporters enter the fort.

1.00pm — PRA armoured cars approach the fort and open fire. Some 20 people die in the shooting and whilst attempting to escape; there is minimal and short-lived resistance to the PRA attack. After surrendering, Bishop, Creft, Whiteman, Norris and Fitzroy Bain and Vincent Noel are taken back inside the fort and shot. Twenty-four-hour curfew imposed; over 100 arrests are made over the following days.

October 20 — General Austin announces the formation of the Revolutionary Military Council (RMC) under his chairmanship. Reagan administration expresses 'grave concern' over events in Grenada and diverts a naval force to the island; the Pentagon prepares its contingency plans for an invasion but does not inform allies. The British Foreign Office reserves comment on developments. Fidel Castro condemns Bishop's murder and Cuba declares three days of national mourning. The dean of the US medical school on the island refuses to declare that his students are in danger.

October 21 — Tom Adams tells the British high commissioner in Barbados that the Organisation of Eastern Caribbean States (OECS), of which Barbados is not a member, is contemplating asking for military intervention. British ambassador in Washington tells US administration that London wants to be informed if the US is taking 'active steps'. The states of the OECS, minus Grenada (Dominica; Antigua-Barbuda; St Kitts-Nevis; St Lucia; St Vincent; Montserrat) meet. The final decision to ask for US military intervention is not unanimous.

October 22 — Eugenia Charles, prime minister of Dominica, phones Grenadian Governor General Sir Paul Scoon; it is later claimed that he asks for 'outside help'. Cuban President Castro sends urgent message to Washington suggesting that the two countries 'keep in touch to avoid violence'; there is no reply. General Austin draws up declaration stating that the US students are safe, that the RMC will be replaced by a civilian administration within 12 days, and that an inquiry into the events of the 19th will be held; Washington later claims that this message was not received until after the invasion. The US government tells London that it has received a firm request for help but that no decision has yet been made. Caricom calls for trade and diplomatic sanctions against Grenada but refuses to back military action.

October 23 — Eugenia Charles formally asks the US for military help in the name of OECS. Two hundred and thirty US marines are killed in Beirut bombing. In Grenada there is no violence; the PRA and militia mobilise to resist an expected invasion. US diplomats meet medical students, only 10 per cent of whom express a wish to leave the island. Scoon speaks to the Commonwealth Secretariat and makes no request for 'help'.

October 24 — 4.00pm Sir Geoffrey Howe informs the Commons that he knows of no intention to invade. Brigadier Rudy Lewis of Barbados is able to visit Scoon, who asks for help but states, 'an invasion is the last thing I want'. In Grenada the curfew has been lifted and some 70 per cent of people have returned to work.

October 25 — 5.40am 1,900 US troops land in Grenada at four points and occupy Pearls and Point Salines airports; 300 Caribbean troops from the OECS, Jamaica and Barbados follow but do not engage directly in military operations. The invaders meet unexpectedly stiff resistance and call in 1,000 reinforcements, including a section of the 82nd Airborne Division, as well as air support. Grenada is bombed for more than a day and a night. Castro receives a reply to his message of the 22nd 90 minutes after the invasion starts; Cuban construction workers at Point Salines are attacked and defend themselves. Over 20 die before they surrender. Howe refuses to condemn the invasion in the Commons.

October 26 — Heavy ground and air attacks continue; at least 30 people die in US bombing of Richmond Hill mental hospital. First group of US students are evacuated under fire; US press prohibited from entering the island.

October 27 — Scoon and wife are released and taken to the USS Guam. US government reports eight North Americans killed and 29 wounded, with 100 Cubans killed and 600 captured; there is no official figure of Grenadian casualties. European reporters challenge US casualty figures and dispute the number of Cubans said to be on the island. Reagan makes a major speech calling the invasion a 'rescue mission' and deriding analogies with the Soviet invasion of Afghanistan; the US government's justification of its operation is expanded to include political factors.

October 28 — Very sporadic resistance; total US troops on Grenada now exceed 6,000. US vetoes UN Security Council resolution of condemnation of the invasion; Britain abstains.

October 29 — US finally permits the International Red Cross to enter Grenada. Bernard and Phyllis Coard are detained; massive airlift into Point Salines begins.

October 30 — Hudson Austin and Selwyn Strachan are detained. US military leaders say they are trying to 'drive the remaining Cubans out of the hills' although Havana declares that all its personnel are accounted for and issues precise lists of those working in Grenada. The US version is maintained for a further fortnight. Every Latin American country, with the exception of Chile, Guatemala, El Salvador and Uruguay, has condemned the invasion. Plessey Ltd confirms that Point Salines was being constructed as a civilian airport. US opens its first diplomatic mission in Grenada.

October 31 — Scoon speaks out for the first time, urging the US not to depart rapidly. Almost all members of the PRA have surrendered.

November 1 — Howe suggests that British intervention was inhibited by the defence cuts he himself imposed as chancellor. In Grenada some telephones and electricity supplies are reconnected and the schools are reopened.

November 2 — Fifty-strong US team running the island under Scoon's nominal leadership. Diplomatic relations with the Soviet Union, Libya and Cuba are broken; Cuba is ordered to withdraw her mission but refuses to do so until all her nationals are repatriated. The Cuban embassy is placed under siege. Nine-ship US task force takes up station in the Caribbean. Several Commonwealth leaders veto the idea of a 'peace-keeping' force under their leadership.

November 3 — Wounded Cubans fly home; US reduces occupation force to 1,500 US troops and 1,500 from the Caribbean.

November 4 — Scoon announces intention of holding elections within a year.

November 15 — Interim government appointed under the chairmanship of Nicholas Brathwaite.

2 Pre-revolutionary Background

Colonialism

For outsiders the turbulent history of the small island of Grenada began with the fierce resistance mounted by some of its earliest inhabitants, the Carib Indians, against numerous attempts at conquest by colonial forces sent from France. The French finally subordinated the island in 1654, when, in a terrible incident that epitomised the fate of the indigenous peoples of the Caribbean in that era, the surviving Indian fighters threw themselves to a collective death over a cliff later named La Morne de Sauteurs (Leapers' Hill), near the present township of Sauteurs. The French proceeded to introduce sugar, slaves, and plantation agriculture. After a century of their rule the island had 82 sugar plantations and over a hundred mills; sugar exports had reached 4,000 tons a year. Grenada had been turned into a small but highly productive factory-farm where none of the original inhabitants remained alive and over 12,000 slaves shipped from West Africa laboured for a population of 1,200 whites.

French rule was interrupted by the British who took control of the island under the terms of the Treaty of Paris (1763) that ended the Seven Years' War. The policy of Grenada's new owners was to accelerate production: by 1774 sugar exports had been doubled and the number of slaves increased to 35,000 so that they now outnumbered their white masters by more than 25 to one. The island also became a trading centre for slaves; during the last decade of the eighteenth century nearly 50,000 Africans passed through Grenada on their way to work in other centres of sugar production.

British policies had the effect of increasing slave resistance, which under the French had been of an individual, sporadic and unorganised character. As early as 1767 the new colonial power was confronted by an island-wide rebellion. However, as was to be the case so often in Grenada's history, events outside the island determined the course of its development. Following the War of American Independence, the British and French empires once again came into conflict and the French re-took Grenada, holding on to it between 1779 and 1783. Although the British retrieved it under the Treaty of Versailles (1783), it was not long before they were gravely disturbed by the effects of the French revolution, which had a considerable influence in the slave societies of the Caribbean. In Grenada the impact of a revolution that proclaimed 'Liberty, Fraternity, Equality' was delayed but exceptionally powerful. In 1795 Julien Fedon, a French creole planter, led a rebellion that took up the slogans and symbols of the revolution in his homeland, drew the support of blacks and whites alike, and succeeded in gaining temporary control over all the island except the area around St George's, the capital. The rebellion was inspired and led by the French planters who had stayed behind under British rule, but it was the slaves who gave it strength and bore the brunt of the 15-month campaign against British forces. Although finally crushed with great violence, this uprising came to be celebrated as the first and most emphatic episode in the Grenadian people's struggle for freedom.

Following emancipation in 1833, the old plantation system entered into sharp decline as the freed slaves sought land of their own. The large estates turned increasingly to share-cropping in an effort to maintain a labour force that always had the option of returning to small subsistence plots in the interior if conditions on the plantations proved unacceptable. As a result of this relatively high availability of land that could be made to yield some crops, wage labour was introduced very late in Grenadian agriculture, only spreading gradually from the 1940s onwards. Even after World War Two Grenadian peasants had greater opportunities to settle on smallholdings than did their counterparts in Barbados or Jamaica. One outcome of this limited but important 'safety valve' was that population movement towards the towns was very low. On the other hand, it should be stressed that the land cultivated by the peasantry for its own use was often of poor quality and the big landlords continued to dominate the countryside. In 1972 farms under five acres in size accounted for 88.7 per cent of total landholdings but only 45 per cent of cultivable acreage. Farms of 100 acres or more accounted for 0.2 per cent of total landholdings and 49.2 per cent of cultivable acreage.

In 1877 the Crown Colony system was introduced and the local assembly controlled by the planter class was disbanded. The result was not greater democracy but more direct control by the Colonial Office in London which appointed and issued orders to the governor. The large landlords did not offer a serious challenge to tighter imperial administration, and the Crown Colony administration languished without serious opposition until 1915, when T.A. Marryshow, a journalist, and C.F.P. Renwick, a lawyer, founded the *West Indian* newspaper. Over the next 20 years the *West Indian* moulded Grenadian middle class opinion and succeeded in aligning that sector behind the call for reforms in the system of government and the creation of a federation of the West Indies. The paper's slogan 'The West Indies must be West Indian' symbolised Marryshow's anti-colonialism and his deep belief in the need of West Indian unity as the means for obtaining self-rule. Two years after establishing the *West Indian* Marryshow and some of his associates founded the Representative Government Association (RGA) to pressure the British for a local voice in the running of Grenada's affairs. The RGA was not radical in its goals or methods but it represented a major challenge to the Crown Colony system and finally succeeded in obliging the British to devolve powers to a local assembly once again.

During a visit to Britain in 1930 Marryshow was impressed by the activities and policies of the Labour Party. Upon returning to Grenada he endeavoured to apply some of these by starting the Grenada Working Men and Women Association, a loosely-knit body that fulfilled some of the functions of a trade union. After a number of initial successes, the Association collapsed through lack of support and unity. Although Marryshow renamed the organisation the Grenada Labour Party and tried to give it a more political character, it lacked a solid basis of support and by 1937 had faded from the public arena. Although Grenada is very small, its working population has always been atomised. Even in 1977 over half of the country's 120 industrial establishments employed fewer than five people and could be described as family workshops; the single largest employer, the brewery, had a workforce of 76 permanent labourers. In previous decades the docks congregated a sizeable number of workers, but even there a lack of formal education, personal connections, and the risks of public association made the labour force reluctant to engage in opposition politics. It was only after World War Two, when appreciable numbers of Grenadians had travelled abroad, if only to the oilfields of neighbouring islands, and the British empire was manifestly in decline at a time of sharp economic crisis, that anything approaching a cohesive working class movement began to emerge and organised political activity developed.

Gairy

In July 1950 Eric Matthew Gairy, a former school teacher who had recently been deported from Aruba for labour agitation, established the Grenada Mental and Manual Workers' Union (GMMWU). The GMMWU was the first union in Grenada's history to organise plantation workers and poor peasants. Established at a time of great hardship due to the depressed prices for the island's export crops, the GMMWU met with an enthusiastic response and grew quickly. When the majority of planters refused to recognise the union Gairy took the unprecedented step of calling a general strike. The support for the February 1951 strike was so emphatic that the local police force proved unable to maintain control, still less frighten the new members of the GMMWU back to work. British naval personnel were brought in from other islands, but their presence only served further to provoke popular anger, which was now brewing up into a challenge to colonial rule itself. Unable to control public order, the authorities attempted to defuse the situation by releasing Gairy from jail, promising to recognise the GMMWU, and offering to negotiate over its demands for pay increases. However, discontent did not die down and the governor was finally obliged to enlist Gairy's support in obtaining calm. In March Gairy made a radio address that effectively halted popular mobilisation and marked the young labour leader's rise to political prominence inside the colonial system. The style he employed was to be typical of his approach over the following 28 years, during which his personality dominated Grenadian political life (see box).

Following the 1951 crisis Gairy became the undisputed hero of the working class and the most powerful trade union leader on the island. He followed what was now an established pattern in Caribbean public life by transforming trade union authority into political influence when he set up the Grenada People's Party (GPP) in 1951. Despite its very rapid formation, the GPP won the 1951 elections, the first to be held under universal adult suffrage, with considerable ease. The party took six out of the seven parish seats, leaving the opposition led by Marryshow and Renwick overwhelmingly defeated.

Exploiting his peasant origins, trade union power and populist style, Gairy entered government with broad backing. However, his administration saw very few changes in Grenadian society and the premier became increasingly divorced from the sentiments of the mass of poor islanders. Always an astute opportunist, Gairy built up strong links with a sector of the agricultural elite; his party — now renamed the Grenada United Labour Party (GULP) — continued to talk about authentic reforms but subsided into a role as broker of political

The Political Style of Eric Gairy

'I feel obligated morally and spiritually to do something to alleviate, to stop, and when I say stop, I mean stop the burning of buildings and fields; interfering with the people who are breaking your strikes — leave them alone; stop taking away things from the estates that are not belonging to you, particularly cocoa and nutmeg. I want you to stop and you must stop now, every act of violence and intimidation . . . I told his excellency the governor that I have gained your respect and your implicit confidence and you will obey me without fail. I, Eric Matthew Gairy, am now making this serious appeal to you to start leading your normal peaceful life. Take my example and be a decent respectful citizen, as I say, starting now. Let me make this point, however, everyone knows that I am a serious young man and when I say "no" I mean "no" and when I say "yes" I mean "yes". Now listen to this: I am searching for gangsters and hooligans, I ask everyone of my people to help me, and if anyone is found setting fire to any place, breaking down or robbing or in any way interfering with people who are working, there will be nothing to save you, because the law will deal with you most severely, and "Uncle Gairy" will turn you down completely. So join me in saying "no more violence'. Come on now, together, "no more violence", "no more violence". Thank you.'

favouritism. In the 1954 elections GULP was returned to power but with a less impressive result and, following the retirement of Marryshow from politics, it came under strong challenge from the newly established Grenada National Party (GNP), led by Herbert Blaize. The GNP claimed to have 'multi-class appeal' and, like GULP, promised wide-ranging reforms even though its principal sponsors came from the commercial sector. Since it was the only real alternative, the GNP defeated GULP in the 1957 poll, the governing party having by now lost its early organisational strengths and attachment to the cause of social and economic reform. GULP had also become immersed in a scandal concerning misuse of official funds which effectively blocked Gairy's return to power for a decade.

Between 1957 and 1967 the GNP ruled Grenada in a lack-lustre manner under the banner of a vague 'nationalism'. The party's policies favoured private enterprise, which was given generous tax concessions, and sought to create a stronger professional middle class in order to reduce the severe imbalances in the island's social structure. In response Gairy returned to his union roots, agitated for wage rises, and progressively chipped away at the GNP's unfulfilled promises to deliver modernisation and independence. Although it did

21

not have an aggressive style, the GNP was locked into the requirements of a precarious agro-export economy; by the mid-1960s it was clear that it would not strike out in a new direction and had settled into an inert and far from impartial system of government. In the face of this stasis Gairy was able to rebuild his popular appeal, and the memory of his own corruption and lack of action faded. Once again, Grenadian politics became organised around the most visible alternative to the government, however questionable the nature of that alternative.

From the late 1950s growing discord between West Indians and the British government obliged the Colonial Office to concede advances towards independence. While the larger and relatively more developed islands, such as Jamaica, obtained full political self-determination early in the 1960s, the small and severely impoverished nations of the eastern Caribbean were led through a graduated administrative process towards full statehood in the 1970s. In the case of Grenada full independence was preceded by an intermediate status known as Associated Statehood, which granted increased powers of self-rule. The 1967 elections were held under this new constitutional arrangement. As a result, when Gairy easily defeated the GNP he became premier with greater powers than ever before. This did not greatly please the British, who were still responsible for the island's external affairs and, in the light of the experience of the previous decade, distrusted Gairy as an erratic demagogue. Yet the consequences of GULP's victory were considerably more severe for Grenadians since the next 12 years of Gairy's government were marked by economic stagnation, domestic repression and personal corruption.

The Rise of the New Jewel Movement

In 1970 Maurice Bishop, the 26-year-old son of a Grenadian merchant who had made his money working in the oilfields of Aruba, returned to the island from his law studies in London. During his stay in Britain Bishop had been influenced by the writings of Nkrumah, Fanon, Malcolm X and Che Guevara, authors who had instilled in the lively young barrister a keen sense of social injustice. Bishop had also been deeply impressed by the Black Power revolts in the US during the late 1960s, and had himself witnessed the Black Power uprising in Trinidad and Tobago in 1970 — an event which was to have great influence over the new generation of progressive thinkers in the Caribbean. Bishop's introduction to Grenadian politics was to be rapid, setting him on a course from which he did not depart despite all manner of external constraints and personal doubts. Shortly after he returned to the island, a group of 22 nurses took to the streets to demonstrate against the state of the general hospital in St George's where there was an acute shortage of medicines and a lack of basic hygiene. Since many people in the capital were aware of the condition in which the hospital was kept, the nurses' little demonstration quickly gathered popular support. Although the crowd was large, the issue on which it was demanding action was both limited and justified, and the government's best course to avoid undue trouble would have been to seek a negotiated settlement. This, though, was not Gairy's style. Fearing even the slightest disturbance of his rule, he set the police against the march and had 30 people arrested and charged. Maurice Bishop acquired his first professional brief under somewhat forced circumstances, but it is likely that he would have taken it on anyway. In a case that dragged on for a full seven months, he and other young lawyers who had been trained abroad under the GNP government and returned to the renewed corruption of Gairy's rule defended and finally obtained the acquittal of all those charged.

Incidents such as these were becoming alarmingly commonplace, but the GNP proved to be as ineffectual in opposition as it had been in government, and Gairy won the 1972 elections without great difficulty. Thus it was in response to the absence of any significant domestic opposition as well as to wider pan-Caribbean currents in favour of political independence, authentic democracy, the improvement of living conditions and the suppression of racism and colonialism that the new generation of political radicals emerged in Grenada. Following Gairy's 1972 victory Bishop joined with another young lawyer, Kenrick Radix, to form the Movement for Assemblies of the People (MAP). MAP was urban-centred and rather eclectic in style, espousing a fervent nationalism and social reforms along the lines of those implemented by Julius Nyerere in Tanzania; it was radical in orientation but not marxist in character. At the same time as MAP was emerging, Unison Whiteman, an economist, set up the Joint Endeavour for Welfare, Education and Liberation (JEWEL), a movement that was similar in style but had a greater following in the countryside, where the majority of the population still lived and worked. In March 1973 the two groups merged to form the New Jewel Movement (NJM), which argued for a series of non-capitalist, state-based measures to rectify Grenada's structural underdevelopment as well as championing economic integration of the Caribbean and opposition to colonialism and imperialism. At the time these policies were not thoroughly developed or integrated into a clear-sighted strategy and the NJM's early success owed much to its concentration on specific problems, such as unemployment and the lack of proper welfare facilities, and its single-minded defence of democratic liberties. The NJM's first manifesto made no mention of socialism (see box).

Introduction to the NJM Manifesto, 1973

'The people are being cheated and have been cheated for too long — cheated by both parties, for over 20 years. Nobody is asking what the people want. We suffer low wages and higher cost of living while the politicians get richer, live in bigger houses and drive around in even bigger cars. The government has done nothing to help people build decent houses; most people still have to walk miles to get water to drink after 22 years of politicians. If we fall sick we catch hell to get quick and cheap medical treatment. Half of us can't find steady work. The place is getting from bad to worse every day — except for the politicians (just look at how they dress and how they move around). The police are being used in politics these days and people are getting more and more blows from them. Government workers who don't toe the Gairy line are getting fired left and right. Even the Magistrates better look out!

The government has no idea how to improve agriculture, how to set up industries, and how to improve the housing, health, education and general well-being of the people. All they know is how to thief the people's money for themselves, while the people scrape and scrunt for a living.'

In the main young, educated and middle class, the NJM leadership lacked established trade union links and the fledgling movement was very small indeed. Yet, by holding frequent public meetings and persisting in showing up the differences between what Gairy said and what he did, it rapidly acquired a popular constituency. In 1973 the major political issue was that of independence, which the recently re-elected Gairy wanted to push through as speedily as possible. Against this plausible policy the NJM raised the demand for 'real independence, genuine independence, meaningful independence', and insisted that Great Britain pay at least US$30 million in compensation for all the wealth that it had extracted from the country during the colonial era. In June 1973, just two months after it was established, the NJM held a 'People's Convention on Independence', attended by over 10,000 people, to denounce the terms under which Gairy was seeking complete administrative autonomy from London. Later in the month party supporters participated in demonstrations against the independence conference taking place in the British capital. On 4 November, the NJM held a second, equally well attended, convention at which Gairy was tried *in absentia* and found guilty of 27 'crimes against the people', ranging from murder to corruption. This meeting, which was attended by representatives of various political currents and social classes, ended with a call for a general strike. In response Gairy made a radio broadcast in which he vowed that he would 'bring the NJM rebels to their senses and wake them up from their dreams in a very short time for 54 different reasons, including sedition and treason'.

Several days after the second convention, on 18 November 1973, six leaders of the NJM — Maurice Bishop, Unison Whiteman, Selwyn Strachan, Hudson Austin, Kenrick Radix and Simon Daniel — went to the town of Grenville to discuss the planned strike with business leaders. Informed of this visit, Gairy attempted to halt the escalation of opposition by resorting to violence. The NJM militants were shot at and then brutally assaulted by the Mongoose Gang, set up by the prime minister in 1967 and led by two notorious criminals who recruited thugs to impose Gairy's wishes when official police action was either insufficient or clearly impermissible. Paid out of the state coffers but without any official status, the Mongoose Gang was responsible for most of the pro-government violence under Gairy and on occasions turned its attentions to members of the police who were reluctant to break the code of conduct inherited from the British. On 18 November the Gang was unusually vicious and some of their victims were beaten unconscious. One account of the incident that has acquired a certain retrospective pathos noted how Hudson Austin nursed a badly bleeding Maurice Bishop on his lap until the blood from his friend's head wounds saturated his shorts.

'Bloody Sunday', as it came to be called, proved to be a serious error on the part of the government and marked a turning point in the development of the opposition movement. This now included a very broad section of Grenadian society, which repudiated the increasing use of violence in a country which, following the abolition of slavery, had an intermittent history but no tradition of repression. With the NJM leadership in jail, where it was left without medical attention for an unpardonable length of time, the anti-Gairy elements of the business class stepped forward and formed a coalition known as the Committee of Twenty-Two. This included the Grenada Union of Teachers, the Civil Service Association, the Chamber of Commerce, some independent unions, all the churches and various middle class groups like the Rotary Club. In no sense could these organisations be labelled left-wing; they had banded together over an issue of fundamental democratic liberty that on this occasion they shared with the NJM. On 19 November the Committee of Twenty-Two called an island-wide strike, demanding that Gairy arrest those members of the police and the Mongoose Gang responsible for 'Bloody Sunday' and immediately dismantle all coercive bodies. Sensing a major crisis in the offing, Gairy quickly agreed to those terms and the Committee called off its strike after a week.

However, with the exception of the formal appointment of an independent commission of inquiry, the prime minister failed to keep the promises he had made in November. The Committee of Twenty-Two and the NJM leadership, now released on bail, called for a new strike beginning on 1 January 1974. This stoppage proved to be highly effective and paralysed the island's economy. Refusing to negotiate, Gairy resorted once again to police action, which greatly increased political tension. On 21 January — 'Bloody Monday' — the police shot and killed Rupert Bishop, Maurice's father, as he attempted to block the doorway of a building where women and children had taken refuge from the violence in the street. The strike lasted three months and was accompanied by frequent mass protests, police violence and popular reprisals against the forces of the state.

In the midst of this crisis Gairy begged Britain for help. The Foreign Office maintained that Grenada's status of associated statehood prevented London from intervening in the island's internal affairs, but the British eventually stepped in with an 'independence gift' of £100,000. This payment enabled Gairy to increase the wages of the civil service and the police and thereby guarantee their support for the government at a time when it was under extreme pressure. Gairy was also greatly aided by the fact that although the country was at a standstill and submerged in a major political crisis, London went ahead in granting independence, which came into effect on 7 February 1974. As predicted by the opposition, independence became a powerful political tool for Gairy, who now projected himself as the 'father of the nation' and exercised unhampered control over all affairs of state. Making use of his entry into the United Nations and the Organisation of American States (OAS), the prime minister denounced his opponents as communists and called for concerted action to be taken against the left throughout the Caribbean. In the same vein the government received military aid from the Pinochet dictatorship and sent men to be trained in Chile as well as establishing close links with the authoritarian regime of Park Chun Hee in South Korea.

After the failure of the general strike, which was finally called off in March 1974, the NJM sought to consolidate itself more firmly and intensified its educational and organisational work. Within two years the party's paper, *The New Jewel,* had expanded its circulation to over 10,000 copies, becoming the most widely read newspaper in an island which, despite its lack of educational facilities, was largely literate. Local 'support groups' were set up in almost every village and held frequent public meetings, although these were sometimes interrupted or broken up by Gairy's supporters. Special NJM organisations were established for women and young people as well as for urban workers and the unemployed. The great majority of people who attended the meetings of these groups were not full party members, but they supported NJM policies and identified closely with its leaders. By 1976 the party had succeeded in securing and broadening its popular appeal and fortified its claim to represent the interests of a broad cross-section of the Grenadian population. Yet it still remained more of a movement than a party in the sense that it was fighting on a clear set of concrete issues but lacked a strategic programme and coherent internal organisation. This state of affairs began to change in 1976 with the return to Grenada of Bernard Coard, a talented economist who had studied and taught in Britain and was a committed proponent of the 'non-capitalist path of development' projected by the Soviet Union and Cuba for Third World countries. More conversant with marxist ideas than those leaders of the NJM who had been politicised on a day-to-day basis and with minimal theoretical study, Coard played a leading role in drawing the party towards official communism.

NJM Statement of Principles, 1976

We stand for:

1. People's Participation, People's Politics, People's Democracy.
2. People's Co-operatives for the Collective Development of the People.
3. Health Care Based on Need.
4. Full Development of the People's Talents, Abilities and Culture.
5. Full Control as a People of our own Natural Resources.
6. Employment for All.
7. A Decent Standard of Living for Every Family.
8. Freedom of Expression and Religion.
9. The Liberation of Black and Oppressed Peoples throughout the World.
10. A United People . . . A New Society . . . A Just Society.

At the time the effects of this shift were not apparent since the formal adoption of 'Marxism-Leninism' was not openly announced. Indeed, the introduction of a model based on the experience of the Soviet party and its teachings were restricted to a very small group that now began to take on a conscious as well as circumstantial vanguard role with respect to the populace that it had succeeded in mobilising over a whole range of issues. Moreover, although Coard had a pronounced influence inside the NJM leadership as a whole and won the admiration and attention of figures whose natural tendencies were towards a form of radical nationalism rather than Marxism, his closest followers initially comprised only one group of a party that had less than 50 full members. This group went under the name of the Organisation of Revolutionary Education and Liberation (OREL), a study group set up in 1976 and which was later to be attacked as a 'party within a party'. The precise status of OREL within the NJM remains obscure, but it is evident that, as befits such groups, it attracted some of the most enthusiastic and impressionable members of the party. Whatever the eventual role of the organisation in the tragic events of October 1983, it is an undeniable and important fact that its supporters played a central part in consolidating the NJM under Gairy and were responsible for many of the accomplishments of the party after it had come to power.

In 1976 neither the internal state of the NJM itself nor political conditions in general permitted more than an initial and uncertain step towards the adoption of demonstrably marxist positions. In line with the broad anti-Gairy policy that the party had been following over the past three years of its existence, it entered the 1976 election campaign as part of a bloc — the People's Alliance — along with the remnants of the GNP and the United People's Party (UPP), which had earlier split from the GNP. The Alliance won 48 per cent of the vote and six seats in the chamber; the NJM took three seats and Maurice Bishop became leader of the opposition. This result was a major achievement since the honesty of the poll was highly questionable. All election officials were government employees, only government candidates were permitted to use loudspeakers or had access to the radio, a great many 'phantom voters' appeared on the government-organised electoral register, and the Mongoose Gang was extremely active in breaking up Alliance meetings. GULP won nine seats and returned to power, but Gairy's legitimacy had been substantially eroded.

Although the opposition denounced the electoral fraud, it did not call for a boycott or refuse to participate in the assembly, on the grounds that it could be used as a forum for criticism of the government and the presentation of alternative policies. This the NJM began to do, but parliamentary opposition had little effect, as the party now learnt through experience. Gairy's response to attacks in the chamber was to impose with vigour the statutes he had already introduced to curb those who held an opinion contrary to his own: the Firearms Act (1968), which rescinded all firearms permits to members of the opposition and made them extremely vulnerable to the Mongoose Gang; the Public Order Act (1974), which banned the use of loudspeakers not authorised by the police; the Newspaper Act (1975), which required a deposit of nearly US$9,000 to be made to the state before publication was allowed and thereby effectively outlawed the popular but impoverished *The New Jewel*; and the Essential Services and Port Authority Acts, which prohibited strikes of any kind in the sectors where the NJM had many followers. As was his custom, Gairy made recourse to cronies placed in control of the trade unions to isolate NJM supporters while employers refused to recognise independent unions and frequently fired their members with the approval of the government.

Apparently oblivious to the mass opposition that he was provoking, Gairy continued to accumulate property for himself, disburse official funds at whim, force sexual favours from women in the civil service, and indulge with great ostentation his fascination with the supernatural. All this was done with little thought to the country's reputation and still less to its depleted financial reserves. Whilst Grenadians might have become accustomed to their premier's antics, such as erecting a massive illuminated cross on a hill top and claiming that he ruled by divine right and 'belonged to the mystical world', it came as some surprise to foreigners to hear him plead in the United Nations for funds to be set aside for 'psychic research' into UFOs or to learn that he was a judge when Miss Grenada won the Miss World contest.

Such behaviour reflected not just an extraordinary arrogance but also the loss of political acumen. As Gairy's activities became more outlandish, the NJM was able to gain important support from those employed by the state who had previously acquiesced in 'Gairyism' but now viewed it as grotesque megalomania beyond all hope of reform. Some of the NJM's key supporters now came from the police force and the army, which had certainly been closely identified with the persecution of the party but were also sufficiently institutionalised for some of their members to hold severe reservations over the government's cavalier attitude to the law. It should also be borne in mind that Grenada is a very small place and that many of these officers knew the NJM leaders personally and were undoubtedly impressed by their middle class backgrounds, high level of education, and commitment to a complete alteration of the island's society based on standards of efficiency and propriety as well as egalitarianism.

These contacts in the security forces proved to be vital to the NJM's eventual capture of power. It was through them that arms were acquired and the rudiments of the party's People's Revolutionary Army (PRA) established. It was also through them that the NJM leadership learnt on 10 March 1979 that Gairy had ordered them to be arrested and 'liquidated'. On Monday 12 March, following the prime minister's departure from the island — which the NJM took to confirm the information it had received — the party decided to launch an all-out offensive against the regime. Early on 13 March some 40 party members took control of the True Blue army barracks and began to mobilise the people by radio. There was a massive response in support, and people took over the island's police stations despite the fact that they were often only armed with knives and cutlasses. Patrols were set up, private vehicles lent, and domestic kitchens opened up for public usage. The entire operation lasted less than 12 hours; there was no concerted resistance and only three people lost their lives, a testament to the leniency as well as the discipline of the revolutionary forces. Of course, in a strict sense this was less a revolution than a popular coup. One day Gairy had been in power facing few apparent difficulties; the next he was gone. For the people of Grenada this was a matter of no little relief and much celebration. The NJM was no less joyous, but it was now confronted with the daunting prospect of taking responsibility for and administering profound social and economic change in a tiny country that was one of the most underdeveloped in the world and inextricably linked to international markets for products over which it had absolutely minimal control. The party fought persistently for its ideals and enjoyed unprecedented popular support, but these now had to be put to the test under adverse circumstances and with little time available for experimentation or preparation. The problems, both obvious and less apparent, were to be legion, but the new government adopted a resilient approach, as personified in Maurice Bishop, who because of his extraordinary popularity and rapport with ordinary Grenadians was the obvious choice as prime minister. Good looking and tall for a Grenadian, Bishop had acquired much sympathy through the loss of his father, who had been a prominent figure, and was widely respected because he had remained in the country from 1973 onwards and dedicated much of his work as a lawyer to defending people of humble background. In some respects his rise to political prominence was not unlike that of Gairy, but Bishop was a convinced radical and although he was from the start the figurehead of the Grenadian revolution, he always presided over a government that was organised along collective lines.

3 The Peaceful Revolution

Building a New Regime

The People's Revolutionary Government (PRG), set up on 13 March 1979, comprised not only members of the party but also trade union leaders, independent professionals and members of the island's business class, such as Lyden Rahmdanny, minister of tourism and connected wth one of Grenada's most powerful firms. There is no doubt that the cabinet was controlled from the start by the NJM, but the government was constructed in order to provide the broadest possible support both at home and abroad. Similarly, the NJM recognised the extreme difficulties involved in making significant changes in the social structure as a result of the miniscule size of Grenada, the largely peasant character of its society, the island's critical dependence upon the export of a few agricultural commodities, and its heavy reliance on imports from and close ties with the Caribbean Community (Caricom) and the economies of the West. Under the inspiration and administrative direction of Bernard Coard, who became a minister of finance as well as deputy prime minister, the government followed the NJM strategy of measured reforms and a progressive rather than abrupt disengagement from the major capitalist economies; the imposition of socialism by decree was also rejected. This gradualist policy, which meant preserving and supporting key sectors of private enterprise, was consonant with the broad character and appeal of the PRG and fully supported by Cuba and the Soviet Union, which base their support for such a policy on the theory of 'socialist orientation' (see box). Although over the short time in which it was applied the policy effected relatively limited changes in Grenadian society as a whole, it registered a sufficiently impressive performance according to purely commercial criteria for the major states and organisations of the capitalist world to desist from launching an all-out offensive against it. Attacks were instead limited primarily to political issues and Grenada's receipt of aid from non-capitalist countries.

Socialist Orientation

The theory of socialist orientation is a reformulated and more rigorous interpretation of the theory of 'the non-capitalist path of development', which from the 1950s was applied by the Soviet Union to a variety of Third World regimes. The theory holds that a direct transition to socialism is not possible in underdeveloped countries, and, as a consequence, a pre-socialist stage, which is neither socialism nor capitalism, must be gone through before a genuine socialist transformation can take place. This pre-socialist period is designated the 'national democratic, anti-imperialist, socialist-orientated' stage of the revolution. The change in definition of this theory from 'non-capitalist path' to 'socialist orientation' was, to a large extent, brought about by the problems associated with its application. A number of regimes hailed as having embarked upon the 'non-capitalist path', notably Egypt under Nasser and Ghana under Nkrumah, evolved in an openly pro-capitalist and anti-Soviet direction. Other regimes became highly repressive and even outlawed the local communist party. Probably the greatest merit of the socialist orientation strategy is its tactical flexibility with respect to alliances between different social classes and in international affairs. For four years the NJM was most adroit in maintaining the support of various classes in Grenada and obtaining assistance and solidarity from international organisations. On the other hand, the NJM also demonstrated some of the contradictions and less palatable features of communist ideology as laid down by Moscow. Bernard Coard, who was the party's chief theoretician and trained most of its cadres in Marxism, clearly had in mind for Grenada a one-party state along the lines of the Soviet model although there would, of course, have been Grenadian peculiarities. Thus, the NJM's somewhat questionable attitude towards such issues as freedom of the press, political detainees and elections can in part be attributed to its inflexible belief in the party as the primary source and guarantor of revolutionary legitimacy. The main theoretical source used by the NJM was K.N. Brutents, *National Liberation Revolutions Today*, 2 vols., Moscow 1977.

After March 1979 the real centre of power in Grenada lay in the central committee of the NJM. Apart from being on the party's highest decision-making body, committee members occupied leading posts in the PRA — which now replaced Gairy's army — and many trade unions, as well as directing the work of the key ministries and the organs of people's power. The political bureau, a sub-committee of the central committee, was charged with developing overall policy, but it was the PRG itself which was vested with full legislative and executive powers and with which Grenadians most strongly identified themselves. Indeed, as later became very clear, many people had no idea who sat on the party's senior bodies or what precise roles they fulfilled.

This subtle but critical elision not just between party and state but also between party and government was evident in other areas. Although it was rapidly acquiring the internal characteristics of a traditional communist party, the NJM joined the Socialist International and gained the open support of European social democracy and other political forces well beyond the official communist movement. Equally, Sir Paul Scoon, who was appointed governor general by Gairy and had previously served his administration in other capacities, was retained by the PRG as the representative of the British monarchy and the island's official head of state. The NJM kept Grenada in the British Commonwealth and Caricom and the country continued to be a signatory to the Lomé Convention.

One of the first acts of the revolution was the suspension of the island's independence constitution. In the *Declaration of the Grenada Revolution,* the PRG pledged to return to constitutional rule at the earliest opportunity and promised to appoint a consultative assembly to draw up a new constitution. In drafting the constitution, the *Declaration* stated, the assembly would 'consult with all the people'; the final draft was to be submitted for popular approval in a referendum. Maurice Bishop also announced that the PRG expected a quick return to 'free and fair elections'. However, this was an issue of some debate inside the NJM, and the PRG refrained from taking any real steps towards the re-establishment of Westminster-style constitutional rule and elections. It did at times reiterate its pledge to hold elections once a new constitution was drawn up, and in June 1981 a constitutional commission was appointed; but the government moved increasingly towards the position that the system of popular power that it had set up was an altogether superior form of democracy to that embodied in the Westminster model. The elections and new constitution were intended to institutionalise the system of popular power. It is worth noting that it was 19 years after the independence of the US (1781) that elections were first held.

Even though popular democracy can be clearly distinguished from formal constitutionalism, it is still not true to say, as did the Reagan administration, that under the PRG there was no constitutional rule. People's Law No.5 of 1979 declared that all pre-existing laws were to continue in force unless specifically repealed or amended. Significant portions of the 1974 constitution were later re-enacted by various People's Laws; others were covered by common law. However, it is the case that the PRG retained extraordinary powers to detain and hold people without trial, and *habeus corpus* was not always respected.

Following the revolution, the PRG arrested and quickly brought to trial members of the Mongoose Gang and the secret police. After a period the majority of those held were released, leaving only the most dangerous still in prison. A number of people were also arrested under the 1979 Preventive Detention Regulation and the 1980 Prevention of Terrorism Law. These acts enabled the PRG to detain without trial individuals suspected of terrorist offences. Although some of the NJM's accusations subsequently proved to be without foundation, a number of those people detained were manifestly involved in conspiracies aimed at toppling the government. These included figures implicated in the November 1979 'De Ravenière Plot', in which some police officers, members of the UPP and right-wing academics working in the US had collected arms and planned to co-ordinate mercenary landings, and members of the 'Budhlall Gang', which in the spring of 1980 mobilised young Rastafarians and attacked army camps. The authors of the bombing of the Heroes' Day rally on 19 June 1980, when three young women were killed, and the assassins of four young men at St Patrick's on 17 November 1980, were not captured, but these incidents gave weight to the PRG's assertions that it faced an internal as well as an external subversive campaign and undoubtedly encouraged it to detain people about whom it had suspicions. Nonetheless, some of those held without trial, such as the ex-NJM leader Lloyd Noel, and the constantly harassed journalist Alister Hughes, were patently guilty of political opposition rather than conspiracy.

Two types of criticism were levelled against the government over the detainee issue. First, organisations such as Amnesty International and the local Catholic church criticised the regime purely and simply for holding prisoners for extended periods without any semblance of judicial process. The PRG responded by claiming that there was a lack of competent lawyers on the island and that the legal system which it had inherited had broken down. The government also maintained that political cases should be tried under the new constitution, a position that was somewhat ingenuous in view of the lack of movement towards establishing a new charter. The second type of criticism was markedly less honourably inspired and emanated from the US government, conservative Caribbean states and the right-wing media, all of which alleged with greater or lesser hyperbole and vehemence that political detainees were being brutally tortured. Church leaders who visited the prison at no stage made any complaint about the treatment of those whose cases they were investigating, and delegations from the Caribbean Council of Churches and the OAS also indicated that they had found no instance of mistreatment. There does, however, remain some doubt over the total number of political detainees; in June 1983 Maurice Bishop gave the figure for those held without trial as 35, but Amnesty considered that there were at least 90 and maybe more.

As with so many other aspects of its activity, the PRG's attitude to political detentions was determined by very real constraints. Although the regime's defence of its need to protect the revolution at all costs manifestly cloaked an aversion to allowing much genuine criticism, subsequent events proved in the most vivid manner that some such protection was indeed necessary. Equally, while Grenada lacked an adequate judicial system of any type, the failure to adopt a measured policy towards domestic opposition rebounded to the government's disadvantage. One critical factor in this regard was the imbalance between the relatively open character of the PRG itself and the increasingly tight and inflexible positions emerging within the party. The contradictions of this relationship did not, however, become clear until forces inside the NJM sought a complete imposition of their party-based conception of discipline and public order on the state. When this occurred, in October 1983, the precedents established by the PRG played an important part in determining how the central committee of the NJM moved against the PRG itself. There was no inescapable logic in this process — prisoners were released at quite regular intervals and the numbers involved in no sense constituted a pogrom — but it is difficult to deny the link.

The PRG also faced international criticism over the closing down of the island's only pro-capitalist newspaper *Torchlight* in October 1979. The government argued with some justification that *Torchlight* had revealed the location of a PRA training camp, had acquired the habit of reprinting anti-PRG articles taken from foreign publications, which often contained libellous and completely untrue material, and manifested a total commitment to removing the new administration. Whether this meant that the paper was, as claimed, working in harness with the CIA, is open to question. The final act which led to the closure of the paper was an article entitled 'Rastas to Protest', which the PRG considered was deliberately designed to exacerbate discontent amongst the Rastafarian community. The PRG subsequently blocked the publication of the *Grenadian Voice,* set up by local businessmen allegedly with the help of outside finance, and the *Catholic Focus,* run by the Catholic church. In defence of these actions Bishop pointed to the 'broad range of views' that were expressed in the government-owned newspaper, the *Free West Indian,* and the existence of a number of papers produced by the mass organisations and the party. The fact that foreign magazines, such as *Time* and *Newsweek,* and newspapers like the *Express* and the *Trinidad Guardian*, were allowed to circulate despite the fact that they were generally highly critical of the PRG provides evidence that freedom of expression through the printed word was limited but not fully suppressed. It should also be noted that Grenadian radios could receive the fiercely critical *Voice of America,* broadcast from Antigua, as well as the stations of other islands controlled by parties far from sympathetic to the PRG. The honesty of news bulletins transmitted by these stations often did not compare favourably with those put out by Radio Free Grenada.

In retrospect it can be argued that the revolutionary regime handled the issue of press freedom clumsily and opened itself to unnecessary criticisms over freedom of expression. There was certainly no lack of such freedom in the streets or at public meetings, at which government ministers would frequently receive extremely candid views from humble folk. However, the NJM was acutely aware of the central role of newspapers such as *El Mercurio* in Chile and the *Daily Gleaner* in Jamaica in destabilising the much stronger left-wing governments of Salvador Allende and Michael Manley respectively. The closure of opposition papers was debated inside the party, but the NJM lacked the confidence or tactical flexibility of the Nicaraguan Sandinista government, which allows the publication of the opposition *La Prensa* even at a time of considerable tension and undeclared war.

It is undoubtedly the case that during its four years in office the NJM enjoyed an effective political monopoly. Shortly after the revolution the GNP had attempted to stage two public meetings, but each was impeded by NJM supporters. Unable to secure some form of recognition from the PRG of its right to exist, the GNP simply disappeared from the political scene. As in the case of the newspapers, if the GNP had been able to mobilise appreciable public support it would not have disappeared without discernible popular discontent. In fact, the NJM's heavy-handed response drew minimal criticism inside the country. This may well not be a valid justification, but it does point to the fact that the free exercise of all liberties by everyone is not necessarily in accord with the popular will. This becomes more readily understandable when one takes into account the fact that for many people in the Third World, like those in Grenada, the formal freedoms of speech, expression and association have rarely been permitted in practice for all the population; instead they are effectively rights for the most privileged sectors alone. Hence, the PRG certainly curbed the voice of those opposed to it, but it also won very wide-ranging support for its view that the voice being curbed was distinguished by its receipt of generous funding from private commerce, powerful international connections and scarcely-veiled antipathy to the revolution. It is relatively easy to raise moral objections to the PRG's stance but much more difficult to stipulate an alternative that would not have entailed a collapse of its authority and the restitution of a different set of freedoms — those determined almost exclusively by economic power.

Popular Power

Probably the most celebrated aspect of the Grenadian revolution was the impulse which it gave to the self-organisation of society at large. As a result of legislation and initiatives made by the NJM there was a prodigious growth in the strength and popularity of the mass organisations — the National Women's Organisation (NWO); the National Youth Organisation (NYO); the People's Revolutionary Militia; the National School Students' Council and the Pioneers. These bodies played a key role in popularising the goals of the revolution, organising voluntary labour brigades, staging literacy campaigns, holding open political debates, and developing the means to resist any armed counter-revolution. It is no exaggeration to say that the popular organisations for the first time permitted the mass of Grenadians to participate in the running of their own affairs. The mass organisations were represented on those state bodies appropriate to each one's specific interest as a means of ensuring that government policies responded to the needs and interests of the population. The leaders of the organisations were also made full members of the PRG.

Under the NJM regime there were eight trade unions in Grenada and most were led by NJM members. People's Law No.29 of 1979 stipulated that workers were free to join the union of their choice, determined by a secret ballot of at least 50 per cent of the employees in each workplace. As a consequence of this law some 70 to 80 per cent of all workers on the island were unionised. The unions remained independent of the PRG and were encouraged to work for the best possible conditions for their members within a framework of free collective bargaining and the market economy. The party newspaper consistently lent its support to workers in dispute with private companies and landlords. However, in order to maintain a favourable investment climate the commissioner of labour was instructed to intervene in disputes that threatened to last a long time. In the great majority of cases this officer was able to force a settlement because of the general support which the unions gave to the PRG. This was not always so, and on occasions those unions which held out for terms that the government was not prepared to concede were attacked for being CIA-inspired or 'ultra left'. Not one, though, was outlawed, intervened by the regime or cowed by force.

By 1978 the NJM had managed to set up a complete network of party support groups in each parish; after the revolution these parish councils continued to function as forums for open dialogue between the leadership and the people. With the influx of participants that these bodies began to attract, a decision was taken to break down each parish into several zones, the country being divided into 36 zones of roughly equal population size. The mass organisations worked in parallel with the zonal councils so that issues of specific concern to any one sector or region were discussed at the monthly workers' parish council meetings or at those of the farmers' group, the NWO and the NYO. The leadership of the NJM as well as of the PRG or government departments participated in these meetings to give an account of their work, explain new programmes or respond to criticism. A cabinet member was usually present at a parish meeting, which had the right to request in advance the presence of any government official that it wished to question.

All major pieces of legislation passed after March 1979 were discussed in meetings of the mass organisations, the process of consultation being built into the PRG's system of popular power. In 1982 this system was widened to include the presentation of the national budget to the people for their criticisms, suggestions and recommendations. This was repeated in 1983. The budget exercise was regarded by the PRG as one of its most pioneering innovations and involved a quite extended procedure. First, expenditure requests from all government departments were studied by the ministry of finance, headed by Bernard Coard. A preliminary draft was then submitted to the PRG cabinet for discussion. This was followed by a period during which officials from the ministry went before the trade unions, mass organisations, zonal and parish councils to discuss the draft with them. The high point of the exercise was the national conference on the economy, which was attended by delegates from all the mass organisations. Breaking up into workshops devoted to specific areas of the economy, the delegates made detailed comments and criticisms on the draft proposals. The budget then went back to the ministry of finance for final revisions and then to the cabinet for approval. Finally, a detailed report was made to the people by the ministry and an explanation was given as to which recommendations had been rejected and why.

Even in an economy as small as Grenada's the elaboration of a national budget is a highly complex affair and not naturally conducive to exhaustive public debate in all its details. Yet the exercise of open deliberation did have an important effect on the development of policy in general and served to imbue ordinary people with a legitimate sense of participation. The fact that such a method of decision-making was a great deal more than more demagogy can be seen in its application to the maternity leave law. A draft of this statute was discussed in all the popular organisations and encountered limited but strong opposition from the teachers' representatives, who proposed amendments that effectively excluded women education workers from the law's provisions. These amendments were, as a consequence, included in the law until a pro-NJM slate won the elections in the teachers' union and obtained a reversal of their organisation's previous policy.

Under the PRG the government of Grenada was not strictly 'constitutional', but it did embody considerably greater popular participation than allowed for, and still less realised, in any of the Westminster-style systems working elsewhere in the Caribbean. These are constructed around a formal apparatus in which positive popular participation is restricted to a single act — that of voting — every few years. In Grenada there was, by contrast, a form of continuous direct democracy. This particular pattern of popular consultation was practical because of the miniscule size of the island, which meant that it was physically possible for the people to have a close dialogue with the leaders and scrutinise major pieces of legislation. In a society which historically had provided no real avenue for democratic debate the system aroused considerable interest and enthusiastic participation. The mass organisations covered over a quarter of the total population and the parish councils were always well attended. By 1983 there was some evidence that levels of commitment and participation had fallen off somewhat as the initial impetus of the 1979 revolution waned, the changes it had wrought became 'normal', and expectations were toned down by economic difficulties and external pressure. However, this quite predictable development was of a social rather than political character; while it posed problems for the PRG, it also reflected the regime's success in establishing itself as the norm rather than an exciting aberration. In this sense it was neither surprising nor a backward move that Maurice Bishop proposed to institutionalise the local councils as part of the country's government.

The system of popular consultation and debate inside the NJM's Grenada evidenced some problems and required a number of refinements, but it was neither the 'mob rule' nor the 'communist dictatorship' claimed by its detractors. Had it been so the PRG would have either failed to exercise authority or been obliged to impose it by force.

In reality, the regime was able to maintain its programme and enjoyed extensive popular support in spite of very harsh economic conditions. It was, moreover, signally devoid of corruption in distinction to almost every other contemporary government in the Caribbean. The onus is quite manifestly on those who attacked this system to prove not only that it was undemocratic but also that it was unpopular and failed to work.

Economic Strategy

In accordance with its interpretation of the theory of socialist orientation, the NJM regime evolved a radical economic strategy based upon the progressive expansion of the activities of the state and the generation of aid and trade links with the East as well as the West. Under the PRG the state sector grew to around 30 per cent of the economy, with the establishment of state enterprises in agriculture, agro-industry, public utilities and tourism. Whatever some local entrepreneurs feared or the US government declared to be the case, the bulk of the economy and its most dynamic sectors remained in private hands.

One central feature of the PRG's economic policy that owed a great deal to Bernard Coard's familiarity with international finance was Grenada's strict observance of the external requirements for the repayment of the national debt. As a result, US efforts to cut off loans, particularly from the IMF and the World Bank, were only partially successful. In March 1981, the US director of the IMF managed to block a US$6.3 million loan for capital projects, and Washington's influence on the World Bank succeeded in halting the disbursement of US$3 million in concessionary funds from the International Development Agency. In June 1981, the US government offered US$4 million to the Caribbean Development Bank (CDB), of which Grenada is a member, but only on the condition that none of the money went to that country. The board of directors of the CDB, the charter of which requires it to make loans solely on the basis of economic need and regardless of political considerations, voted unanimously to reject the grant. Later that month Caricom denounced the US action as 'gross aggression'.

Although the US is the single most important power in the IMF, controlling 20 per cent of votes and well able to organise loan vetoes against the wishes of a majority of member states, it was not able to impose a complete block on funds to Grenada. In part this was because much of the country's borrowing was within its statutory limits and not subject to strict regulation of economic performance by the IMF. Moreover, because Grenada's currency is the Eastern Caribbean dollar (EC$), and its financial affairs are closely linked to those of the other small islands of the region, it was extremely difficult to destabilise its economy without affecting those of the neighbour states, as the case of the CDB loan demonstrates. The PRG was also quite successful in winning support from member states of the IMF, which may have persuaded the US not to insist upon its boycott. It should be borne in mind that at this time Washington was pushing through the IMF large loans to countries like El Salvador, which could not possibly meet the standard financial criteria demanded. In order to give itself some room for making such manifestly political loans the US would, on occasions, be prepared to tolerate lesser sums being allocated to Grenada in a kind of political trade-off. At the same time, explicit US pressure on the EEC to stop the European states making grants and loans to Grenada was often resisted (see Appendix I for the British position). By scrupulously meeting repayment schedules and expanding the economy, so that in 1982 it registered a growth rate of 5.5 per cent, the PRG defied attempts by the international financial agencies to deny it funds. However much the sympathies of those who controlled the IMF and the World Bank lay with the positions adopted by the US administration, and however political the effects of the terms under which they make loans, these bodies ultimately found it exceedingly difficult to reject or ignore the accounts produced by the PRG. As a consequence, they were obliged to continue relations with an extremely well behaved client and even grudgingly offer their congratulations for the performance of the economy under the PRG's supervision. In September 1983 the IMF approved the payment of a loan of US$14.1 million to Grenada on terms which did not impede the PRG's existing programmes and which were markedly less harsh than those demanded of Guyana at the same time.

Coard's approach to the issue of foreign loans and aid demonstrated that in financial affairs at least he was capable of taking a prescient and pragmatic line. Having lived in Jamaica between 1974 and 1976, he had witnessed the bauxite companies destabilise the Manley regime, and he had closely studied how economic sabotage had been undertaken by the multinationals, banks and the US government in Guatemala (1950-54) and Chile (1970-73). Coard identified one of Grenada's few advantages in the international field as lying in the fact that less than 3 per cent of its imports came from the US and none of these was of strategic value. Also, there were no US-owned banks in the country, the major foreign bank being

Barclays. However, the island's economy was critically dependent upon imports, and the PRG's ambitious programmes required a high level of state investment and therefore foreign borrowing. Initially quite large sums were received on soft terms from European governments, the non-capitalist countries and members of OPEC. Yet by 1981 these were insufficient for the maintenance of the government's plans for infrastructural development. When asked by a Nicaraguan interviewer why Grenada had had recourse to the 'monster' (IMF) in its search for capital, the minister of finance offered a far from doctrinaire response:

'Where else were we to obtain funds? The point is this: the private banks lend money at very high levels of interest, much higher than those of the IMF, which are fixed. The private banks increase their interest rates. A country can be completely paralysed if a loan is contracted at 9 per cent and then you have to pay it back at 20 per cent. Against this you have to consider the conditions and demands made by the IMF. We have presented four programmes to them. In two cases we accepted their conditions and twice we rejected them. It's quite straightforward.'

As a consequence of increased inputs of capital from various sources government spending rose significantly, from EC$8 million in 1978 (EC$2.6 = US$1) to EC$16 million in 1979, EC$39.9 million in 1980, EC$79.2 million in 1981, and EC$101.5 million in 1982.

The lion's share of capital expenditure was earmarked for the construction of a new international airport at Point Salines. This project was central to the PRG's plans to boost Grenada's tourist and agricultural industries. Its importance for the tourist trade is critical since the existing airport at Pearls cannot accommodate the large aircraft used by the principal holiday carriers and does not possess facilities for night landing. Travellers to Grenada have, therefore, to transship in neighbouring islands, such as Trinidad and Barbados, which had governments far from sympathetic to the PRG. To the fury of the US government, a confidential IMF document written in June 1983 supported the PRG's view that the construction of the new airport was critical to the economic development of the island.

In agriculture the PRG first concentrated on improving the efficiency of the 25 estates which had been inherited from the Gairy regime. A number of advances were made and subsidies were even cut back, but in 1983 most of these farms were still operating at a loss because of the effects of hurricane damage and the depressed state of the international market for Grenada's essential exports. Between 1979 and 1980 nearly half the island's banana crop and a quarter of cocoa production were lost as a result of inclement climatic conditions; total losses were estimated at US$20 million. In 1980 the international price of nutmeg, cocoa and bananas fell by an average of 22 per cent.

In April 1983 the PRG began to acquire additional agricultural estates under the Land Utilization Law, passed in September 1981, which gave the minister of agriculture the power compulsorily to lease for 10 years on favourable terms the idle portions of farms over 100 acres in size. As a result of this measure and the outright purchase of other properties, the state came to own some 30 per cent of the island's cultivable land, an appreciable advance towards the NJM's ultimate objective of eliminating the planter class completely. However, agriculture was no longer the power base of the local capitalist class, which derived most of its wealth from commerce and tourism. Many of the estates taken into state control by one means or another were badly run down and very few were making a profit. In general, expropriations were given little or no publicity and were rarely resisted strongly by landlords, many of whom were relatively powerless and lacked a united organisation with which to defend their properties. This had been evident under Gairy, who had brought some 10 per cent of the country's cultivable land under state control and distributed most of it to his followers. Under the PRG there was no programme of direct distribution of lands to individual peasants. However, the government greatly increased credit facilities for small farmers and for the first time provided a guaranteed market for crops other than nutmeg, cocoa and bananas; this was part of the policy of diversifying Grenada's marketing structure. Some success was registered in reducing unemployment through the establishment of co-operatives in agriculture, fishing and handicrafts, but these organisations did not really begin to flourish before the NJM was removed from power.

In banking the PRG purchased two of the island's four foreign-owned banks, and by 1983 the state-owned banks controlled some 45 per cent of all deposits. In tourism a state sector was created on the basis of the hotels and guest-houses previously owned by Gairy; in 1983 the government bought the island's biggest hotel, the Holiday Inn. At the time of the October 1983 coup the tourist industry was just beginning to pick up from the trough it had experienced after the revolution because of the world recession and adverse publicity in the US. The prioritisation of tourism in the economic strategy of the regime gave the revolution a particularly congenial character and fitted in with the image of the 'peaceful revolution'. On account of the island's natural charm and the PRG's anti-imperialist stance, Grenada became an important venue for radical debate on Caribbean politics and a conference centre for progressive organisations from the US and elsewhere. Finally, the agro-industrial enterprises established by the

PRG proved to be highly successful. For the first time in the island's history there was local production of saltfish, smoked herring, nutmeg jellies and fruit juices. The relatively rapid and profitable adoption of these processing industries was viewed as an excellent start to the process of diversification away from simple cultivation.

The relationship between the PRG and the private sector was always contradictory. Contrary to its policy for agriculture, the government actively encouraged greater private investment in manufacturing and tourism, and as a result of the overall economic growth brought about by its infrastructural programme and improvements in financial planning, the merchant class was able to increase its profit margins. Some of its sections openly supported the PRG despite their apprehensions about the NJM's marxist ideology. Moreover, the government provided a number of direct incentives to local entrepreneurs, leading to an appreciable upturn in private sector activity in areas such as beverage production, agro-processing, furniture and garment production and flour milling. On the other hand, some Grenadian capitalists adopted various techniques for disguising the real extent of their profits and began to syphon their capital off abroad. Although tourism was Grenada's largest earner of (invisible) exports, profits remained modest and under the PRG investment in the private sector fell sharply. Moreover, while the state did not take over any of the country's relatively powerful merchant houses, the PRG substantially increased taxes on imported goods and services, thereby incurring the hostility of many businessmen. The subsequent division of the entrepreneurial class into those who could perceive the benefits of having a government anxious to continue and expand production and those who feared that it would sooner or later expropriate their property was not unpredictable. Whatever may have been his intended policy, Bernard Coard publicly stated on many occasions that government participation in any sector of the economy could not exceed some 30 per cent without having an adverse effect on prices. Although the PRG did have a greater share in tourism and plantations, it otherwise publicly maintained the position adopted by the minister in March 1979:

'From the first day we were clear with them (local entrepreneurs). We told them that they had a role to play in the economy and society. We made it clear that the days of controlling the island's politics had come to an end and that from now on it was the day of the masses, of the majority. So, they had to limit themselves to economic activity, to making money. But making money according to the rules and regulations which defend the rights of the workers: the rights to association, unity and unionisation, price and quality controls etc. On that basis they could make a profit on their investments, they could contribute to the construction of the economy, develop the productive forces of society, increase employment possibilities, spend or invest their profits as they saw fit.'

Although the construction of the airport at Point Salines was understood by the Grenadian people to be highly important to the country's economy — indeed, in a way it embodied all their hopes for the future — the real popularity of the PRG's policies lay with their commitment to providing the rudiments of a welfare system. The social reforms enacted from March 1979 onwards certainly required increased foreign borrowing and greater aid, but they provided a tangible improvement in the quality of life and represented a substantial advance for a small and impoverished society.

The PRG made all medical care free, expanded health centres and increased staff so that, while still insufficient, the ratio of doctors, dentists and nurses to the population was markedly improved. In the space of four years six new dental clinics were built, new casualty and X-ray clinics constructed, and Grenada acquired its first eye clinic. Access to secondary education was greatly broadened with the reduction of fees from the equivalent of US$26 a term first to US$4.50 and then to nothing at all. School milk and lunches were provided free by the state for the first time. The Bernadette Bailey School was constructed — the country's second senior school in 350 years — and university scholarships abroad were increased from three under Gairy to 220, although there were not enough students able to take them up. The island's housing stock was improved, less by new construction than by an extensive renovation programme. By 1982 this had cost nearly US$1 million and included the homes of over 20,000 people, nearly a fifth of the population. According to government figures, 50 miles of road were built, the output of electricity increased by more than 40 per cent, and piped water made available to 50 per cent more people than had access to it before the revolution. Those in greatest need of these facilities were not made to pay for them; 30 per cent of Grenadian workers were exempted from paying income tax after 1979 and family allowances were increased.

Confrontation with Washington

Under the Carter administration the US initially adopted a wait-and-see attitude towards the PRG. The overthrow of Gairy was widely welcomed in the Caribbean and the US State Department was unsure what direction the revolutionary government would take. Furthermore, the revolution occurred at a time when Washington was still floating the idea of a degree of reconciliation with radical regimes in the Third World. Although the National Security Council forwarded the idea of blockading the island, this was not considered a tenable option at that stage. Nevertheless, relations between St George's and Washington deteriorated very quickly once the PRG established close relations with Cuba. As early as 10 April 1979 Frank Ortiz, the US ambassador to the Eastern Caribbean, informed the PRG that the US would 'view with displeasure any tendency on the part of Grenada to develop closer ties with Cuba'. Taking exception to the Cuban connection, the US turned down Grenada's request for defence aid and offered a paltry sum in economic assistance. In response to this attempt to dictate policy Maurice Bishop made the first in a series of strong defences of Grenada's right to self-determination and an independent foreign policy:

'From day one of the revolution we have always striven to have and develop the closest and friendliest relations with the United States, as well as Canada, Britain, and all our Caribbean neighbours . . . But no one must misunderstand our friendliness as an excuse for rudeness and meddling in our affairs, and no one, no matter how mighty and powerful they are, will be permitted to dictate to the government and people of Grenada who we can have friendly relations with and what kind of relations we must have with other countries . . . We are not in anybody's back yard, and we are definitely not for sale. Anybody who thinks they can bully us or threaten us clearly has no understanding, idea, or clue as to what material we are made of.'

From this point on US hostility towards the PRG increased, and relations became markedly worse when Grenada failed to vote against the Soviet invasion of Afghanistan in December 1979. According to the *Washington Post,* this caused the Carter administration to discuss for the first time the use of covert operations against the PRG. In the event they were not taken up, but the US government did approve the adoption of propaganda measures, leading to an increase of anti-Grenada articles in the North American press. Typical of these was an editorial published by the *Washington Star* in August 1980:

'Grenada, the newest recruit to the ranks of the leftist governments in the Caribbean, has become a training ground for terrorists of many nationalities. Members of the Baader-Meinhoff group from Germany can be found there, along with Russians, Jamaicans, PLO Palestinians, and a sinister English-speaking group known as the machete terrorists because, as the African Mau-Mau once did, they mutilate their victims.'

Denial only served to endow malicious concoctions such as this with an importance they did not merit, but there can be little doubt that they helped to accumulate a perception amongst the populace of the US that Grenada, wherever it might be, had joined the ranks of the 'enemy'. Lacking any meaningful resources to reply but undeterred, the PRG's foreign minister, Unison Whiteman, continued to implement the NJM's foreign policy in the UN and other international forums. The government backed the PLO's right to an independent sovereign state as it did that of the Polisario Front in the face of Moroccan occupation of the Western Sahara. It also supported the Heng Samrin government in Kampuchea — the US continues to back the Pol Pot forces — but voted against the Soviet Union in the UN over the Korean airliner affair.

With the inauguration of Ronald Reagan a qualitative shift in the US attitude to Grenada took place. In line with the new administration's belief that almost all instances of disagreement with Washington — however slight or profound they might be — were a function of 'Soviet expansionism', Grenada became a domino. Along with Cuba and Nicaragua the island was portrayed almost exclusively as a source of regional unrest and an 'exporter of revolution'. Despite the fact that 130 US cities had a population greater than Grenada, the US armed forces were 2,350 times larger than those of the island, and the US economy 27,520 times larger, the Reagan administration made an absolutely minimal effort to enter into peaceful co-existence with the PRG. Efforts to deny Grenada funds had only limited results, but the campaign to sabotage the tourist industry was more efficient. Numbers of visitors dropped by some 10 per cent, and a sample poll of 40 travel agents in the Washington and New York areas revealed that 90 per cent of them advised that Grenada was an 'unsafe destination', having been given this advice by the State Department.

The administration's policy of expanding the CIA and increasing its illegal activities did not affect Grenada as directly as it did Nicaragua since in 1981 the Senate Intelligence Committee rejected an Agency plan for a complete covert destabilisation operation. Nonetheless, this did not mean that the CIA was prohibited from undertaking activity on the island, merely that it was denied the funds for extensive activity. Thus, although there is no concrete proof that the Agency was involved in the June 1980 Queen's Park bombing or other conspiracies, such involvement cannot be entirely ruled out, especially since it is in the nature of CIA activities that their authorship is exceptionally difficult to substantiate. The idea that all opposition to the PRG was orchestrated by the Agency is difficult to accept, but it is highly unlikely that US intelligence personnel were not involved in some of it or were completely absent from the island before October 1983, when their presence is beyond all reasonable doubt. The idea that the CIA is a consistently efficient and successful organisation rests very largely on the impact of its operations in Chile, Guatemala, Guyana and, to some extent, present-day Nicaragua. Yet a great deal of its activity, however unpleasant, retrograde and illegal it might be, has proved to be highly inefficient. In the case of Grenada the results of internal destabilisation were not very rewarding and seemed to offer few prospects of success in the medium-term, if only because of the absence of a significant anti-PRG constituency. This undoubtedly played a part in turning Washington's attentions primarily to external propaganda and military activity.

The most sustained US proganda offensive against the Grenadian revolution centred around the construction of the new international airport. The fact that this was primarily — but by no means exclusively — in the hands of the Cubans drew an angry response from Washington, which persisted in describing it as a potential military base for the Soviet Union. By 1983 the administration's claims had become sufficiently extravagant for the airport to be linked to another threat — a planned base for missile-carrying Soviet submarines. Such installations existed exclusively in the imagination of the US government. It was alleged that the new airport's runway was much longer than required by ordinary commercial jets and that its strategic location made it ideal as a refuelling stop for Cuban troops on their way to South America and Africa. In a remarkably restrained response, the PRG pointed out that many Eastern Caribbean islands, Antigua, Curaçao, Barbados, Guadeloupe, St Lucia and Trinidad, had runways of equal or greater length than that planned for Point Salines. It was also noted that although the bulk of the construction work was being undertaken by Cuban workers, plans for the airport had been approved by the EEC, which had also partly financed the project. Moreover, much of the technical work had been contracted out to Western companies: the Layne Dredging Company of Florida, Plessey Airports Ltd of Britain, and Metex of Finland. The EEC and Plesseys later joined with the PRG to issue explicit denials of US charges that the airport was being built to military specifications (see box). At the same time, journalists and politicians from the US and elsewhere were invited to visit Grenada, see the airport and assess the position for themselves.

In addition to economic, political and propaganda campaigns, the Reagan administration ostentatiously developed contingency plans to invade Grenada and overthrow the revolutionary government by force. In September 1979 Maurice Bishop had strongly criticised the Carter government's decision to establish a mobile task force in the Caribbean as a result of Washington's 'discovery' of Soviet troops in Cuba when, in point of fact, such personnel had been stationed on the island for over a decade to the full knowledge of the US government. In November 1980 a large US naval exercise code-named 'Solid Shield 80' caused appreciable anxiety in Grenada, but it was under Reagan that such activities became significantly more ambitious and

Point Salines

The dispute over the character of the new international airport being built at Point Salines existed well before 1983. Ex-Secretary of State Alexander Haig publicly opined that the runway was a potential base for 'every aircraft in the Soviet-Cuban inventory'. However, the dispute became a critical issue for US policy when, in March 1983, Ronald Reagan himself addressed the question in his celebrated 'Star Wars' speech that outlined plans to build a space laser 'umbrella' against hostile nuclear missiles. During his discourse the screen behind the presidential podium showed aerial photographs of the airport site. The president, referring to 'the rapid build-up . . . of military potential' in an island 'which hasn't even got an airforce', strongly implied that Point Salines formed an integral part of an international threat to US national security. Departing from his prepared text, Reagan declared,

'Grenada is building a new naval base, a new air base, storage bases and barracks for troops, and training grounds. And, of course, one can believe that they are all there to export nutmeg.'

In case anybody might be so misguided as to nurture such a belief, it was later pointed out in briefing session that the 'naval facilities' at Calivigny Point 'far exceed the requirements of that tiny island'. This statement was made by Nestor Sanchez, deputy assistant secretary of defence for inter-American affairs, ex-employee of the CIA, and a veteran of the abortive invasion of Cuba at the Bay of Pigs. There are no 'naval facilities' at Calivigny. There is an undeveloped inlet according to both British Admiralty charts and Richard Lundgren, executive vice-president of the Layne Dredging Company of Hallandale, Florida, which in 1982 dredged some coral from the inlet to a depth of 20 feet. Only yachts and small fishing vessels can enter the bay without having their keels torn away. The camp at Calivigny does possess a rifle range, garages, sheds and an obstacle course; it was the training centre of the army of a sovereign state. In reiterating the president's claims over Calivigny, Fred Ikle, deputy secretary of defence for planning, described only the camp's obstacle course as 'Soviet-style'. The nuclear threat posed to the US by this obstacle course may be assessed from the hillside overlooking Calivigny without the assistance of satellite photography.

Responding to the charges made by President Reagan and his defence staff, Dessima Williams, Grenadian ambassador to the OAS, denied any military developments in the country other than those designed for its defence against external attack. Ms Williams described the claims made about Point Salines as 'not only provocative but utterly fatuous'. The PRG reiterated at length and in detail its declaration that Point Salines was a civil site essential to the development of Grenada's economy. Similar statements were made by the EEC and the Layne Dredging Company. On 1 November 1983, following the US invasion of Grenada and its conversion of Point Salines into a military base, Plessey Ltd issued the following statement:

'Plessey Airports has temporarily withdrawn the majority of its employees from the construction site of the international airport at Point Salines, Grenada, pending clarification of future policy. Employees have returned to their homes in the UK.

'In view of many statements which have been made, some with little basis in fact, the following facts are relevant:

'The airport was designed to facilitate the economic development of Grenada, especially with regard to tourism. It would enable direct international flights by wide-bodied jets to Grenada without transfer through other Caribbean countries. It was also designed to satisfy a diversionary airport requirement for other Caribbean countries.

'The runway is 9,000 feet long by 150 feet wide and is designed to the standards and practices of the International Civil Aviation Organization. It would enable a Boeing 747 with a full load short of seven passengers to take off for a flight direct to London. Fully comparable runways exist in Antigua, Jamaica, St Lucia and Barbados, where the runway is 11,000 feet long. Factors governing the length of runways for civilian aircraft relate primarily to payload and range at take-off and local climatic conditions.

'The terminal building was designed to accept a peak flow of 350 passengers per hour, corresponding to the arrival of one Boeing 747. Floor space is 8,000 square metres against the FAA standard of 10,000 square metres, the lower figure adopted in Grenada being acceptable outside the US. It includes a duty-free shop, catering facilities, passenger handling facilities, baggage reclaim facilities, flight information systems, full customs facilities, gift shops and boutiques. It is designed to luxurious standards, with landscaped surrounds.

'Navigational equipment does not include radar. Prevailing climatic conditions at Grenada allow Visual Flying Rules for most of the year.

'A military airbase would require the following facilities, none of which exist at Point Salines:

'— parallel taxiway;
'— arrangement for dispersed parking;
'— radar;
'— hardened aircraft shelters for protection against bomb blast;
'— secure fuel farm (i.e. underground);
'— underground weapons storage;
'— surface-to-air missile sites or other anti-air defences;
'— perimeter security;
'— operational readiness platform with rapid access;
'— aircraft engineering workshops and major stores;
'— aircraft arrester gear.'

Following the US invasion the director of tourism of Nicholas Brathwaite's Washington-backed government declared, 'The international airport is key to any real viable tourism development.' Since 25 October 1983 Point Salines has, of course, been a US military base.

threatening.

In August 1981 the US led the largest naval exercises conducted by Western forces during peacetime since World War Two. Code-named 'Ocean Venture 81', this exercise deployed over 120,000 troops, 250 warships and 1,000 aircraft in a fictitious scenario that had NATO forces battling Soviet ships in the South Atlantic, Caribbean and North Atlantic before finally vanquishing them in the Baltic. A central component of the exercise was the invasion of a Caribbean island group known as 'Amber and the Amberines'. (Grenada's formal title is Grenada and the Grenadines; a locality near Point Salines is called Amber.) Staged at the island of Vieques, off Puerto Rico, this phase of the manoeuvres had the 'hostile' forces of Amber (backed by 'Red', presumably Cuba) seizing US hostages, refusing to negotiate, and compelling a US invasion. At the time the scarcely-veiled threat to Grenada was widely appreciated. Subsequent US naval exercises in November 1981 ('Red X 183') and March 1983 — when US craft came within six miles of Point Salines — must leave even the most sceptical with the distinct impression that the final, real invasion of October 1983 was not only carefully planned, but had also been rehearsed on several occasions.

In response to the political offensives and the open threat of military intervention the PRG mounted a diplomatic counter-offensive. For this it found friends and a hearing in the Commonwealth, the Socialist International, and the Non-Aligned movement as well as in the non-capitalist states and left-wing currents throughout the world. Inside Grenada the government was particularly courteous to visitors and pointed to the presence of a private, US-owned medical school, the St George's School of Medicine, to show that the PRG was not anti-American. Students at the school played sport with Cuban construction workers from the airport and even received lectures from Cuban doctors. Staff at the school were voluntarily informed by Cuban officers as to how many civilian and military personnel were on the island and to what extent Havana had provided the PRA with arms. All this information was substantially at variance with the aptly titled 'guestimates' publicised by the US State Department, but it subsequently turned out to be remarkably accurate. Had the US government been engaged in a genuine intelligence operation rather than one of outright deception it would presumably have drawn reports on Point Salines from the North American students who went jogging there every morning.

Although the PRG scored a number of successes in the propaganda battle over the airport, it felt obliged to enhance the island's defences. Many young people joined the militia, membership of which was voluntary, and exercises became more frequent in the spring of 1983

51

although at any one time only a few units were fully armed. It is possible that the extensive mobilisation of the PRG's limited military resources prevented a mercenary landing, which was the form of attack most feared. None occurred and if one had taken place it is likely that the PRA and militia could have defeated it. Yet the exchanges of the last fortnight of March were far from a simple bluff on either side; following Reagan's 'Star Wars' speech the state of alert decreed by the PRG was observed with an authentic sense of emergency. For a number of weeks, rather than days, it was expected that the island would be attacked.

Once the furore over the airport had died down somewhat and the PRG's mobilisation of the PRA and militia had been reduced, Maurice Bishop made a major diplomatic initiative by visiting the US in June in an endeavour to improve relations. President Reagan refused to see him, and the Grenadian prime minister had to be content with a conversation with William Clark, Reagan's national security adviser.

The visit apparently did nothing to assuage Washington's ire at having in the Caribbean another 'domino' against which it could only level pitifully feeble charges. The US government had failed to agitate internal discontent through the creation of opposition newspapers or political parties, and it had reaped poor results from imposing diplomatic isolation and an economic boycott. Having failed to convince Congress of the merits of a covert destabilisation campaign, the administration was obliged to rely on military exercises and menacing statements. Despite the fact that much of its cold war rhetoric was treated with incredulity outside the government's die-hard followers, the threat it posed was very real. Yet it also seemed to be based on an 'all or nothing' understanding of foreign relations, and until October 1983 very few people genuinely believed that even the Reagan regime would risk the formidable diplomatic problems of launching a full-scale invasion of an independent and sovereign state. If any country was likely to fall victim to such a move, it was thought to be Nicaragua, which presented a much greater military challenge but had been the object of a prolonged propaganda campaign, a major CIA covert operation, and an extensive US military build-up on its borders.

The second, far less obvious, failure of Maurice Bishop's trip lay in its contribution to the breakdown of trust and unity inside the NJM itself. As Bishop later revealed, the party leadership had debated whether the trip should be made for a week, and the final decision had not been unanimous. It was, perhaps, the last party decision in which the prime minister won the argument. Although it was never openly cited as a cause for complaint by those who were increasingly at variance with Bishop's political style, the feeling that he was shying away from a firm and uncompromising stance against the US gained currency in these circles. It was claimed by independent sources after the US invasion that Bishop's trip had indeed marked the opening of a rapprochement, but no substantive evidence has been presented to support this view, which runs counter to the logic of previous and subsequent developments. However, Bishop's trip was an undoubted success in terms of swinging public opinion in the US in favour of the PRG and therefore in weakening the Reagan government's attacks against it. Bishop, who understood the importance of public opinion much better than did Coard and his group in the NJM, was in this sense at least able to counter the threat of an invasion within the US itself without actually negotiating with the administration. It was the reversal of this more favourable attitude inside the US towards the PRG that enabled the Reagan government to stage its invasion. The value of this admittedly intangible factor was not registered by powerful figures inside the NJM over the summer of 1983, by which time suspicions over precise nuances of policy had acquired great importance and provoked internal difficulties and disputes that a more experienced and less embattled party might well have overcome without great problems.

4 Collapse of the Revolution

Crisis of the Party

The leaders of the Grenadian revolution displayed a sober appreciation of their chances of withstanding a total US invasion. Maurice Bishop and his comrades knew that any major assault would be successful but they promised a resistance that would tax the invader and leave an important example to other anti-imperialist movements. In the event, stern opposition to the US occupation was mounted by the PRA and elements of the militia. The tragedy was that, whatever they believed, these young people were not defending the same revolution which the great majority of the Grenadian people had supported. The regime that confronted the US invasion bore little relation to that which over the previous four years had done so much to antagonise Washington. It was a militaristic rump of both the PRG and the NJM, a six-day dictatorial regime founded on the collapse of the government led by Maurice Bishop.

The Reagan administration quite naturally made maximum advantage out of the collapse of the revolution, citing it at one stage as the sole cause for an honourable and humane intervention, a 'rescue mission' in more ways than one. Subsequently the invaders and those small Caribbean states that acted in harness with them pointed to a manifest lack of opposition to their actions from the Grenadian people to rebut criticisms that they had made a mockery of the UN charter, acted outside international law and revived the most arrogant and archaic form of imperialism. This was the saddest and most bitter aspect of the invasion for those who sympathised with the Grenadian revolution. It had imploded, turning upon itself before the marines arrived, and that implosion constituted little less than an invitation to invade. Much of the confusion surrounding these events endures, but it is an unalterable fact that the internecine strife inside the NJM and the subsequent assassination of Maurice Bishop and a number of his comrades was not just a political error of enormous proportions or a grossly misconceived application of 'Leninism'; it served to bring the whole revolutionary process to an abrupt and bloody end. It is possible that the events of October correspond to more than just the pressure of the US diplomatic and economic embargo on Grenada, but until theories of conspiratorial activity are given substantive proof one must accept the tangible evidence that the revolution fell apart largely because of the problems that existed within it.

Even in the immediate aftermath of the collapse it was clear that there was no simple cause. The dispute revolved around the personalities of Maurice Bishop and Bernard Coard, but it also involved much broader political issues. It was not essentially about ideology, but it did centre on political tactics and party discipline, which inevitably helped to draw out and sharpen incipient differences of style, approach and strategy. What was initially a question of party organisation and discipline developed into a crisis for the government and then the country as a whole. This combination of factors and developments reflected more than anything else the enormous difficulty of transforming with sensitivity but firmness a small and vulnerable society.

Although in a country the size of Grenada strong personalities have a substantial influence on public affairs, the personal characteristics of Bishop and Coard were less important in themselves than for what they represented. Maurice Bishop was always more than a figurehead. For most Grenadians he symbolised their revolution and was their trusted 'chief'. Even those who opposed him never denied that Bishop was an exceptionally engaging man, possessed of a great talent for mixing with all layers of society, making cogent and fiery speeches, and ever disposed to listen patiently to the complaints and suggestions of ordinary folk. Bishop was, in short, a charismatic figure and an accomplished populist politician. His sympathetic character made him a natural mediator and gave the PRG a flexible and accessible image that did much to commend it to those who harboured reservations about its policies. In this sense Bishop represented an individual bridge not just between the government and the mass of Grenadians but also between the NJM and the PRG, which, it must be remembered, contained non-party members and did not work openly towards the full party programme but only those parts considered applicable to the strategy of socialist orientation. This bridge eventually collapsed because the prime minister's attributes did not fully meet the requirements of the party, which correctly identified its leader's failings but completely undervalued his talent for maintaining popular support. Bishop was certainly not a highly disciplined man and proved to be a poor administrator. Moreover, although intelligent and highly motivated, he was not a theorist or strategist and was prone to 'follow his nose' in political affairs. In many instances this gave the NJM a considerable advantage but it was also an impediment for a party seeking to map out a strategy, consolidate its internal cohesion and broaden its membership and influence. By mid-1982 some leading members of the NJM felt that dependence on the prime minister's tactical skills and natural popularity was hindering the development of their party. They perceived that they had a leader who possessed some but not all of the attributes of a revolutionary leader. Furthermore, if the existing situation was not rectified the threat of 'one-man-ism' or personalist rule would become a reality.

Bernard Coard was in many respects the antithesis of Bishop. Learned and retiring, even brusque, he was no less hard-working or dedicated to the revolution, but principally concerned with planning, administration and ideology. An unkempt and plump figure, Coard had none of the ostensibly natural features of a revolutionary leader and never sought personal popularity. He was in a sense removed from many of his comrades both by the fact that he was an intellectual and a theoretician and because he had not been in the island in the early 1970s, when the NJM was founded and engaged in its most taxing campaigns against Gairy. The fact that his wife, Phyllis, was a Jamaican and not widely viewed as a sympathetic figure helped to maintain this sense of distance that in a society like Grenada can have a discernible effect. Coard's particular responsibilities lay in economic management and the development of the NJM from a heterogeneous grouping of radicals and nationalists into a disciplined vanguard party founded on Marxism-Leninism. His direction of the economy was, given the objective constraints and consciously imposed limits of the strategy of socialist orientation, predictably pragmatic and yielded significant positive results. However, in terms of the party, the strategy allowed far less flexibility and actively encouraged a sharp disciplinarian approach intended to pave the way for the NJM's eventual political and organisational domination of public life. Thus, while the NJM maintained the appearance of being a very active but open body, leading but not completely dominating the government and the state, the party's objective was to become a vanguard organisation with just such control. Although the NJM did indeed already control the apparatus of the state, and particularly those sectors concerned with security, its progress towards a greater political influence in the country was impeded by the same factors that demanded a flexible economic policy: a dependent and highly vulnerable economic structure; a low level of political education; and massive external pressure. In attempting to overcome these problems, the NJM came increasingly to develop an understanding and internal application of Marxism that was hierarchical, schoolbookish, and narrowly centred on the power of the state. Stress was placed on 'Marxism-Leninism' as a fixed science, which was handed down by the party leadership and uncritically consumed by the rank and file. Coard was the prime mover of this system, which was not entirely out of keeping with his character but above all else reflected the political exhaustion and personal exasperation of a small group of highly motivated people attempting to change society against considerable odds.

All examples of political and social change go through different stages and watersheds that relate both to the ideas and abilities of those leading the political movements concerned and to the objective conditions under which they take place. The Grenadian revolution was no exception in this respect, experiencing a considerable impetus in its early stages and then tailing off somewhat in energy and direction as it confronted a new set of problems that required resolution in a manner significantly different from that in which the revolution was made. While Maurice Bishop represented the kind of outlook that makes revolutions and makes them popular, Bernard Coard was more attached to the tasks of their subsequent consolidation. It was for this end that he had established OREL and sternly tutored its handful of members in the theory of Marxism, understood as a scientific system that, if applied with vigour and rigour, could overcome the most insuperable problems. The precise membership of OREL remains obscure, but it is evident that by mid-1983 the central committee of the NJM was dominated by its approach. This may well have been less because members of the shadowy organisation had a majority on the party's leading body than because, at a time when the party was experiencing tangible problems, their steadfast and unified attitude, facility with the language of Marxism and close links with Coard gave them a distinct advantage over militants who shared many of the same beliefs and objectives but acted themselves with a flexibility that they perceived the NJM needed if it was to retain any popularity.

It was only in September 1983 that the issues in debate inside the central committee came to centre on the composition of the NJM leadership and the personalities of Maurice Bishop and Bernard Coard. Over the preceding years — even before 1979 — the two men had co-operated closely and harmoniously and defended one another when they came under criticism. This collaborative approach began to fracture in October 1982, when Coard insisted on resigning from the central committee and its political bureau on the grounds that he was excessively overworked and obliged single-handedly to develop and administer party and government policy. Coard's position was that if he continued to fulfil this role the revolution would be placed in an extremely vulnerable position because should he die or disappear nobody could adequately replace him. Arguing against Bishop's position that he should stay on the central committee and continue his educational work there, Coard said that it would be 'petty bourgeois' to take this 'easy way out' and that the central committee had collectively to fortify itself in terms of theory and political strategy. Being supported by his closest admirers — notably Leon Cornwall, Ewart Layne and Liam James of the PRA and Selwyn Strachan, the minister of mobilisation — Coard was able to retire from the NJM leadership. He remained deputy prime minister and minister of finance but was to serve officially in the party leadership again only for a few weeks before the US invasion; after October 1982 his role in NJM affairs was to be that of an *eminence grise* operating behind the scenes and only occasionally attending formal meetings to which he was specially invited. James, Layne and Chalkie Ventour — all close to Coard but also hard-working members who deserved their positions — were elected to the political bureau while Kenrick Radix was dropped from the central committee because, it was believed, he was not dedicating himself to study in line with the decision fully to adopt 'leninist standards and functioning'.

It is conceivable that Coard's resignation signalled the first move in a deliberate plan to curb Bishop's authority by placing Coard outside of policy-making spheres and therefore in a good position to re-enter the arena when matters went awry, as he warned they might. It can, however, be presented equally convincingly as the move of a prescient and tough politician anxious to school his colleagues through experience. In all events, the resignation did not arouse great suspicion, notably cool relations, or significantly alter the outward image of the revolution. Its main impact was inside the central committee itself, which, whatever Coard's knowledge of its deliberations or contact with its members, began to approach the party's problems in an almost panicky manner.

The internal state of the NJM by the summer of 1983 was certainly poor. Its total membership was not more than 300 militants, many of whom were 'candidate members', still in the process of receiving political education and lacking full voting rights in accordance with the organisational traditions of leninist parties. Since the NJM was not just a left-wing party but one which governed a country, its low membership in a society of 110,000 people is remarkable. It confirms that the party continued to repudiate easy populism and membership for its own sake, and that it adhered rigidly to the concept of a 'vanguard organisation'. However, the membership was not just low but also declining. This was principally because of the enormous demands made of militants, whose party, civic and governmental obligations as well as their ordinary work kept them tied to 14-hour days six days a week. The strains that this timetable imposed were evident in the high incidence of illness at all levels and the growing inefficiency of political and other work. It was noted in several meetings of the central committee that important members of the NJM were drifting away because their obligations had exhausted them beyond all endurance. As a result, the vigour and sensitivity of the NJM's activity in the unions and mass organisations had fallen off, according to the consensus on the central committee, to a critical degree. There was resistance to the popular education programme, a falling away of the membership and enthusiasm of the NWO and NYO, an increasing incidence of tactical mistakes, and a 'general drift' in the NJM's work that substituted genuine political leadership with brow-beating obligation. Although some of these features were evident from the outside, the central committee seems in retrospect to have appreciably exaggerated their scope and implications. It was not apparent that the revolution was in grave and immediate danger from within. This, however, was the line taken by a section of the central comittee and, whatever the underlying cause, such an understanding dominated its proceedings in 1983.

The Debate

In July the central committee confronted what it perceived as an incipient crisis by holding an extended extraordinary session at which the progress of the NJM and the revolution was assessed. This meeting led to extensive self-criticism and the implementation of a variety of administrative changes, but both were essentially superficial and conducted in a coded manner that suppressed real political differences. No major changes came about despite the formal candour of the admissions that the party was facing severe difficulties. The central committee's appraisal of the period since Coard's resignation was that it had made partial gains but that the structural problems remained.

These problems were translated from the NJM as a whole into its leadership at a further extraordinary meeting of the central committee held from 14 to 16 September. This meeting had been convened to analyse the results of the decisions made at the July

59

meeting, and before long the debate turned into a discussion of the leadership and how it might be reorganised (see Appendix 2). The debate centred on a proposal made by Liam James that the lessons of the recent period could only be properly applied if the leadership was divided between Bishop and Coard with both retaining their state positions but Coard taking full responsibility for organisational work and chairing the political bureau. Coard would return to the central committee but Bishop would continue to chair it and sign all documents as well as retaining his post as commander-in-chief. The minutes of this meeting show that Bishop, although taken aback by this move, did not reject it out of hand. Indeed, he initially acquiesced in the implicit critique of his performance and promised to consider the proposal, which on paper seemed a reasonable suggestion for ironing out the imbalances in party and state organisation. Outright opposition came only from George Louison, the minister of agriculture, who did not reject James's assessment of the relative merits of the NJM's two leading militants but argued that it would be extremely difficult to make the plan work in practice. Unison Whiteman, who was also close to Bishop, was less forthright in his reservations whilst General Hudson Austin, the PRA commander who was reckoned to be closer to Bishop than Coard and who had just returned from North Korea and missed the early part of the discussion, also reserved judgement and abstained. The minutes show that many members of the committee were already aware of the proposal and supported it in a uniform, almost orchestrated fashion. The discussion was marked by a consistent employment of abstract marxist terminology that rarely touched on concrete issues. Tension increased markedly when, after the better part of 15 hours' talking, Louison failed to gain any formal recognition, let alone support, for his view that whatever the formal merits of the proposal, it was going to be extraordinarily difficult to implement in practice. After a strong intervention by Louison, Bishop himself began to emphasise the fact that the motion amounted to a vote of no confidence in him. The prime minister backed away from acceptance, finally agreeing only to consider the proposal. In the final vote Louison was alone in offering opposition; Austin, Whiteman, and Bishop, who was in the chair, abstained. The meeting ended in a heated atmosphere with Bishop declining to be present on the 17th when the central committee discussed the proposal with Coard. In the event, that meeting included only Austin of those who had not originally supported the power-sharing formula; Bishop, Whiteman and Louison had left on a trip to St Kitts. Coard stated that he would await Bishop's decision, but that his conditions for acceptance continued to include the distribution of central committee minutes to all members of the party, a move to

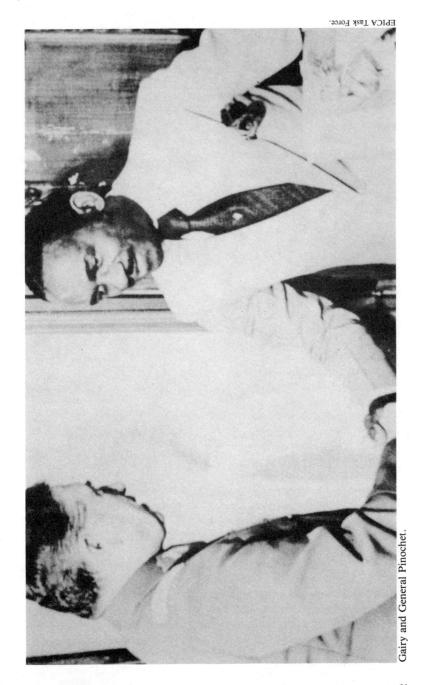

Gairy and General Pinochet.

61

Maurice Bishop.

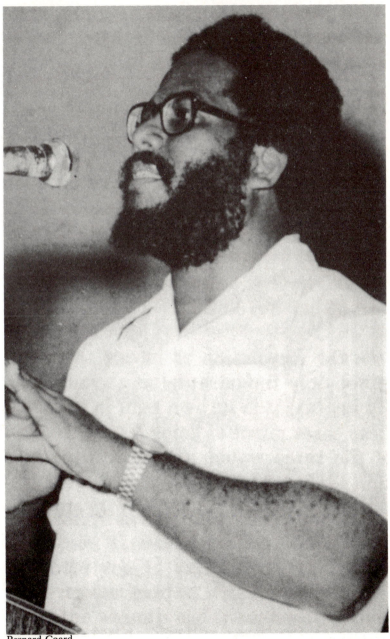

Bernard Coard.

Road repairs.

Point Salines airport under US occupation.

REWARDS

By Using Your

TELEPHONE
HOT LINE

To Authorities

To REPORT WEAPONS AND AMMUNITION which
been hidden and CUBANS who are still hiding out
authorities.

A REWARD is being offered for information.

$ EC 264.00 for functional weapons
$ EC 1320.00 for Cubans hiding out
Just tell authorities where to find them and collect the
reward. Your name will not be revealed.

The government of Grenada and the Caribbean Peacekeeping Force have set
up a telephone HOTLINE for your use. Call 3205 .... Also,
information of this sort may be given at the Army Claims Office in St. George's
and to Caribbean Peacekeeping Force Personnel or U.S. military personnel.
Your Name will be protected, if desired.

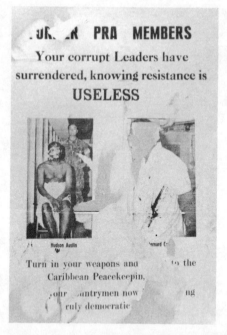

FORMER PRA MEMBERS

Your corrupt Leaders have surrendered, knowing resistance is

USELESS

Hudson Austin   ...rnard C...

Turn in your weapons and ... to the Caribbean Peacekeepin...

...our ...untrymen now ... ...ng

...ruly democratic

US marines at breakfast. The picture depicts the collective suicide of the Caribs at Sauteurs.

which Bishop was strongly opposed as liable to prejudice open discussion but which Coard insisted upon as necessary for party democracy.

On 23 September the prime minister did not attend a central committee meeting called to hear his decision on the power-sharing formula. It was said that he was ill, but most probably he felt unable to address the question in a decisive fashion. On the 25th Bishop refused to attend a meeting of the whole party called to discuss the matter. He said that he had personal problems, that the central committee already knew his position, and that he needed more time to think the matter through. The meeting refused to accept these excuses and a five-person delegation eventually managed to persuade Bishop to come since Coard had refused to attend if he was not there. In the meeting the great majority of speakers attacked the prime minister's behaviour and attitude and supported the central committee's proposal for joint leadership. George Louison, Bishop's strongest supporter, was not present. At the end of nearly 15 hours of debate, 48 full members of the NJM voted overwhelmingly to implement joint leadership, which some speakers referred to as 'collective leadership' and others appeared to confuse with it. The speeches had a major impact on Bishop, who as the minutes relate, made a complete self-criticism and fully accepted the final vote:

'Cde Bishop stands and embraces Cde Coard. Cde Bishop said that it was correct for him to come to the General Meeting and stay and hear the views of the party membership. He said that reflecting in isolation would not have been correct for him since he would have seen things in a lopsided manner. He said that the entire General Meeting had accepted the Central Committee analysis and decision and this has satisfied his concern. He admitted to the General Meeting that his response to the Central Committee criticism was petit bourgeois. He said that the General Meeting has rammed home that the criticism was correct and so too was decision. He said "I sincerely accept the criticism and will fulfil the decision in practice".

'Cde Bishop went on to say that his whole life is for the party and revolution and the difficulty he had was because so many things were going through his mind. He said that he agreed with Cde Moses Jeffrey that he had not shown confidence in the party. But all these things are now behind his back. He said that today is indeed an historic day and a break with the past. He said that the party comrades are maturing and are capable of taking strong positions. He said that his desire now is to use the criticism positively and march along with the entire party to build a Marxist/Leninist party that can lead the people to socialism and communism. He pledged to the party that he would do everything to erode his petit bourgeois traits. He said that he never had difficulties in working with Cde Coard and joint leadership would help push the party and revolution forward (applause).

'At the end of Cde Bishop's speech the entire General Meeting broke into singing the Internationale and members filed past to embrace Cdes Bishop and Coard.'

Despite this remarkable public about-turn it is clear that when Bishop left shortly afterwards for a two-week trip to eastern Europe he still had grave doubts about joint leadership. The prime minister's behaviour throughout this period was akin to that of a man without firm direction and deeply disturbed by events taking place around him. His failure to adhere to an agreed timetable, attend meetings or fully respect the protocols of the party as well as his changes of position must have told against him with the membership as a whole. Yet, while they conducted themselves in a formally correct manner, the majority of the central committee had acted with such uniformity and insistence that the minority, and especially Bishop himself, could legitimately suspect that a power struggle was in the offing. It is probably for this reason that the prime minister sought time and space in order to make a major decision over the future of the Grenadian revolution. The erratic response made by Bishop suggests that the matter had gone beyond mere discussion between comrades and had become a manoeuvre in which political power was at stake. The advantage possessed by those who wanted to alter the nature of the revolutionary leadership was that they possessed a large majority on the central committee and the support of the membership. They could, therefore, operate strictly according to party rules. Bishop, on the other hand, outnumbered and confused, saw himself losing control and was unable to present a coherent case either for himself or for a policy of strengthening the NJM's links and popularity with ordinary Grenadians. It should be borne in mind that all the participants knew each other extremely well and had exhibited a high degree of fraternity and solidarity over the years. As a result, the new situation must have been very disturbing and unfamiliar.

In retrospect, it is clear that the absence of Maurice Bishop, Unison Whiteman and George Louison from the country for a fortnight marked a critical watershed in the development of the party crisis. During their absence Major Leon Cornwall, a firm supporter of Coard's, returned from Cuba, where he had been ambassador, to take up his post in the command of the PRA, which was given a long-awaited pay rise. This move strengthened the position of the central committee in the army, whose chief of staff, George Louison's brother Einstein, was attempting to mobilise support for Bishop. The central committee also received reports that George Louison had discussed the crisis with Grenadians in Europe, which was construed as an important breaking of party discipline despite the fact that the issue had been debated with NJM militants in Grenada. Even greater alarm was sown inside the committee when the touring party stopped off in Cuba on its way home. There Bishop was met at the airport by Fidel and Raul Castro and eight other members of the Cuban central committee. This was an unusually high-powered group for such a short visit by a close and familiar ally; it aroused suspicion that Castro was not only signalling to St George's that he supported Bishop, a personal friend, but that he was also advising him. The Grenadian party leadership subsequently sent a message of protest, but both Bishop's supporters and Castro himself deny that any discussion of Grenadian internal affairs took place. All the same, it is apparent that the central committee majority had cause for concern, and it is certain that the Cubans were aware of the problems. The outcome was that when the touring party returned to the island, positions had hardened.

When Maurice Bishop arrived at Pearls airport he was met only by Selwyn Strachan, as significant a departure from protocol as was the prime minister's reception in Havana. According to George Louison, Bishop told Strachan that he wanted a review of the leadership question to be on the agenda of the central committee meeting on 12 October. This seems to have been interpreted by Strachan as the prelude to outright rejection; it was reported back as a negative response and must have been construed as an effort to challenge and reverse official party policy. Henceforth the debate became a dispute and extended well beyond the leadership question.

Matters came to a head on Wednesday 12 October. At 7am the PRA, in which Coard had a dominant influence and which contained many central committee members, held a meeting at which a strongly worded resolution attacking 'right opportunism', in a clear reference to Bishop, was passed unanimously. This motion was carried to the political bureau at 8am, but it was not debated because a separate, more immediate, issue had arisen. On receipt of an accusation from one of the prime minister's security guards that Bishop's head of security, Cletus St Paul, had been spreading rumours that Bernard and Phyllis Coard planned to kill Bishop, the political bureau called the sentries off Bishop's house and placed them under the authority of the central committee. This move finally broke the illusion of unity and was the first concrete measure to separate Maurice Bishop from the apparatus of government. The accusation concerning the assassination rumour was then taken up by the central committee itself, which met at 3.30pm. At this meeting Bishop was asked to deny the rumours on Radio Free Grenada (RFG); he did this but the broadcast was not repeated, and the lack of clear news caused widespread confusion and concern. Coard was not present at the meeting and the joint leadership was not discussed.

The accusation that Bishop had spread the rumour of his planned assassination may well not have been a fabrication. Yet it should be noted that such rumours had appeared before, and during the prime minister's absence such talk had prompted Bernard Coard to leave his house, which was next door to Bishop's. Bishop was not informed of this until he returned and no concrete evidence for the plan had been presented. If external forces, such as the CIA, intervened in the crisis, the spreading of this rumour or the accusation that the rumour was being disseminated may well prove to be a key piece of politically-motivated disinformation. Whatever its provenance, on 12 October it was the central committee that benefited from it.

The precise timing of Maurice Bishop's house arrest is unclear, but it certainly took place before the afternoon of 13 October and may have occurred late in the night of the 12th. What is clear is that Bishop did not speak, as Austin later claimed, at the meeting of the entire membership of the NJM held on the afternoon of the 13th. There was minimal opposition at that meeting to the motion that Bishop be expelled from the party and stripped of all his positions. Those who were present say that the tenor of this meeting was quite abnormal for the NJM, being highly virulent and very antipathetic to the prime minister. Although the central committee declared that no action should be taken until an inquiry had been held into the rumour accusations, the party as a whole seems to have lost any conception of the gravity of its decisions. Nonetheless, it was responding to a leader who had initially not rejected the idea of joint leadership but merely expressed reservations, later withdrawn these and fully accepted the proposals, and later still raised further doubts and reservations. It was these reservations and their implications for party discipline that the membership of the NJM was due to hear and discuss on the 12th, when the question of the assassination rumours emerged. However perplexing these developments might have been, they themselves did not provide a basis on which Bishop and his supporters could be accused of 'right opportunism', a charge against which they had been given no opportunity to defend themselves. Moreover, the prime minister had now been detained and effectively deposed on the basis of a serious but unsubstantiated accusation, reflecting preference for the word of a junior security officer over that of the head of the revolution. However questionable the procedures of the NJM, they manifestly did not permit such actions to be taken. More importantly still, by taking such measures, the central committee displayed a quite impressive failure to perceive their impact on the populace at large. If there was any conspiracy it was handled with incredible ineptitude; if there was none the upper echelons of the NJM had lost their nerve and taken most of the party rank and file with them.

There is no doubt that the majority of the NJM supported the actions of the 12th and 13th, but on the 14th they were brought face to face with the consequences of these actions. Selwyn Strachan went to RFG in an attempt to explain the situation; he was immediately chased off the premises and threatened with violence. Elsewhere other sharp rebuffs were administered to party militants. In the midst of the confusion, which by now had been relayed to the outside world, a number of impromptu demonstrations for Bishop's release took place, but there was no violence. At the end of the day Coard, whom Strachan had previously declared to be the new leader, announced his resignation ostensibly to rebut rumours that he had staged a plot and was indeed planning Bishop's assassination. Repeated statements that Bishop was safe at home did little to calm the tension.

On Saturday 15 October Kenrick Radix and Norris Bain, who had already resigned as ministers, organised a small demonstration in St George's. This evaporated without incident but afterwards Radix and others were arrested, which halted negotiations over the crisis between George Louison and Unison Whiteman, who still held their posts and were seeking a settlement, and Selwyn Strachan, who was acting on behalf of the central committee majority. Coard encouraged these talks but rejected any Cuban involvement in mediation; the Soviet Union resisted becoming involved and the Nicaraguan government failed to make an initiative before it was too late.

The weekend produced no shift in the central committee's position, reflecting its belief that it could sit the crisis out, allow the people to exhaust themselves and wait for Bishop to concede on the most important demands. There was no violence and only a few arrests had taken place; on the face of it matters seemed containable. Late on Sunday 16 October, General Hudson Austin made a major speech on RFG when he announced that the party was going to set matters straight and that it hadn't done so before because of the need to maintain unity. According to Austin the major problem was that Maurice Bishop refused to accept the principle of collective leadership. This speech was the fullest public explanation of the central committee's position.

The central miscalculation made by those who arrested Maurice Bishop concerned the response of the people. For better or worse, the majority of Grenadians saw Bishop as the symbol of the revolution and, being largely ignorant of developments inside the party, understood only that, out of the blue, their leader had been jailed on the basis of rumours about a planned political killing. Since killings of any type were an extreme rarity on the island, such a charge carried considerable odium, and the fact that it was treated seriously by Bishop's own comrades made it all the more repugnant. At no stage was there any popular acceptance of the case made by the central committee, which committed a fundamental error in identifying the party with the people when, in fact, there was an enormous distance between them. The committee also miscalculated in its assessment of Maurice Bishop's likely response to the situation in which he now found himself. Although nervous and emotional, the prime minister did not capitulate but hardened his position. In effect the central committee had by its precipitate executive action left him with no alternative but to resign or fight the matter through to the end. External mediators, such as Trevor Munroe of the Workers Party of Jamaica, pushed for his acceptance of the central committee's terms but met with no success. There was no indication that the committee was prepared to settle the crisis on any terms other than its own.

According to George Louison, he (Louison) met with Bernard Coard on 15, 16 and 17 October but received no tangible response from the central committee. Coard told him that they did not fear the popular response, his exact words being reported as:

'. . . they can stay on the streets for weeks; after a while they are bound to get tired and hungry and want peace . . . Williams did it in 1970 (in Trinidad), Gairy did it in 1973 to us in St George's, and it can be done again.'

On Tuesday 18 October, Louison rang Coard and told him that he would wait no longer and that since the central committee had all the power it was up to it to make some concessions. Coard replied that there would be no response before 2pm on the 19th.

On Wednesday 19 October — the last day of Bishop's life — a final effort was made to avoid a complete breakdown in the revolutionary government. At 6.30am Louison was permitted to meet Bishop in order to discuss with him the committee's demands that:

1. The NJM should remain on a socialist path and Maurice Bishop should do nothing to alter it.
2. Maurice Bishop accept the principles of criticism and self-criticism and democratic centralism.
3. Bishop accept that the state is subordinate to the party.
4. The post of commander-in-chief be abolished and military affairs be directed by the central committee.
5. Bishop accept responsibility for the crisis.
6. Bishop remain prime minister, an ordinary militant of the NJM, and only attend political bureau meetings for consultations.

These terms signified that Bishop's removal from real power was intended by the central committee, which was now manifestly under the leadership of Bernard Coard and no longer seeking the joint leadership originally proposed by Liam James on 15 September. The two final points were rejected outright by Bishop and Louison and the fourth was questioned. After nearly two hours' discussion the two decided that their minimal position should be that the prime minister return to the central committee and the political bureau. They asked the committee to set up a new mediation team, to lift the detention order on Bishop and allow him to make a public statement.

These counter-proposals were never discussed because of mass action. On Tuesday 18 October schoolchildren had occupied Pearls airport chanting 'no Bishop, no school' and some people had been detained. At the time it was widely rumoured that a further demonstration would take place in St George's on the next day. In the event, this was led by Unison Whiteman, who had rejected an offer of political asylum from Barbadian premier Tom Adams and returned to the island at the height of the crisis. Between 9am and 10am perhaps 3,000 people marched to Bishop's house and released both him and Jacqueline Creft after the few guards on the building had failed to put up any real resistance. Bishop did not make any statement and was clearly in a very nervous state; he was smoking heavily, though this was a habit of his, and he had not been on hunger strike. It seems certain that, having been released with remarkable ease and as a result of the action of a large crowd of people, the prime minister decided to mount resistance to the central committee. Together with his closest supporters — Unison Whiteman, Vincent Noel, Jackie Creft, Norris and Fitzroy Bain — and a large crowd, he made his way to Fort Rupert, where there were some scuffles with the sentries but no fighting took place.

There remains considerable doubt over the nature of this demonstration since some participants carried pro-US placards and others were known to be opposed to the NJM. While honest supporters of the PRG clearly constituted the majority of the crowd, the presence and intentions of others have led some commentators to suggest that it was at this stage that CIA involvement played an important part in determining the course of events. At the time the presence of some people was suspicious enough to persuade a number of Maurice Bishop's supporters, such as Einstein Louison, to refuse to participate. Certainly, the central committee was not telling complete untruths when it later asserted that there were counter-revolutionary slogans being shouted and members of the bourgeoisie present in the crowd. Although there is no proof, it would not be surprising if the CIA had a role in this; it had been given plenty of time to prepare and had an interest in encouraging a violent conflict within the ranks of the party and the PRG.

Having taken charge of Fort Rupert at around 11am, Bishop and his supporters occupied the PRA's communication centre there, sent out for more arms, and attempted to negotiate with the army commanders by radio. No statement was issued to the outside world and no agreement was struck with their opponents. At around 1pm three PRA armoured troop carriers arrived outside the fort, where a large crowd was now congregated. Without any warning, the PRA began firing at the crowd and the building. At first their fire was returned and three soldiers died, but the PRA clearly had the advantage and once it was plain that they were disposed to kill unarmed civilians, Bishop ordered a surrender. The firing had lasted for some six minutes and an estimated 20 people died, some of them in attempting to escape by jumping over a nearby cliff.

The shock caused by this event may be judged from the fact that at first the crowd thought that the soldiers were coming to join them and then that they were firing blank rounds; it did not enter their heads that the soldiers would fire live ammunition at them, and this caused a critical delay in the dispersal of the crowd. Having retaken the fort, the PRA ordered everybody to file out at gunpoint. All were allowed to go free except for Bishop and his five most prominent supporters, who were taken back inside. At approximately 1.40pm, 20 minutes after the fort had been retaken, a further, short burst of gunfire was heard. The prime minister and his followers had been executed, in cold blood and, most probably, following discussions between, at the very least, senior army officers. However, no senior political or military figure was seen at the fort during these events; the operation was under the direct command of Captain Lester Redhead. Maurice Bishop's last reported words were, 'the masses, the masses'. The only published comment made by Bernard Coard after his capture by US forces was that he was not responsible for Bishop's death. It is too early to assess what truth such a statement might contain. What is certainly true is that both Maurice Bishop and members of the masses died at the hands of the army, which had been established to defend them and now took power under Bernard Coard's direction.

Military Rule

During the six days between Maurice Bishop's death and the US invasion, confusion and fear reigned in Grenada. The killings of 19 October were a terrible shock for a population that under Gairy had become accustomed to general thuggery and corruption but had little or no experience of cold-blooded political assassination. The fact that a much-loved prime minister had been killed by his own comrades in the name of a revolution he supposedly led made this shock all the more traumatic. General Austin's address on RFG late on 19 October did nothing to calm the state of extreme nervousness or clarify the situation. No attempt was made to deny that Bishop was dead or to pretend that he had not been at odds with the central committee and the PRA. Austin limited himself to reiterating the party's charges against the prime minister and asserting that the 'counter-revolutionaries' had launched a well-organised military rebellion, which was very far from the case (see box).

Having failed to win popular support for their cause during the week of Bishop's arrest and having very nearly lost all control of the island on 19 October, the new rulers immediately adopted dictatorial measures. Late on that day an indefinite 24-hour curfew was declared, effectively placing the entire population of Grenada under house arrest while the PRA began an island-wide search for supporters of the late prime minister. Over the next three days up to 150 people were detained by the security forces in an unprecedented operation that further increased confusion and tension. Although the measure did allow the central committee to control public order and put an end to demonstrations, it also served to harden feelings and build up a sense of extreme apprehension which was eventually to manifest itself in the demonstration of relief and approval when the US invaded.

The curfew gave people time to reflect upon the events of 19 October. It also deprived most of the population of an opportunity to provide themselves with food and water. Even the burial of many of those killed around Fort Rupert was obstructed, further sharpening feelings of grief and outrage.

On Friday 21 October General Austin announced the formation of a Revolutionary Military Council (RMC) under his chairmanship. This 15-strong body included almost all the leaders of the PRA, amongst them Colonels James and Layne and Major Cornwall, the leading critics of Bishop in the central committee, six members of which served in the new government (see Appendix 7). The most notable absence was that of Bernard Coard, who was, nevertheless, thought to be directing the affairs of the regime although he made no public appearance after 14 October. The establishment of an exclusively military regime combined with the curfew and wave of detentions appeared to signal the end of the revolution even though Austin and others reiterated that it would be carried on in the name of the NJM.

While Grenada existed in a state of suspended animation, outside the island matters were moving rapidly to a head. On 20 October the US government made a public expression of its 'grave concern' at events, and President Reagan redirected a naval taskforce on its way to Lebanon towards Grenada. The US press and the government itself began to refer to the PRG as 'leftist' and the new rulers as 'marxist', a subtle but important change of nomenclature that indicated the

Statement issued by General Hudson Austin,
19 October 1983

Revolutionary Soldiers and Men of the People's Revolutionary Armed Forces: Today our People's Revolutionary Army has gained victory over the right opportunist and reactionary forces which attacked the Headquarters of our Ministry of Defence. These anti-worker elements using the working people as a shield entered Fort Rupert.

Our patriotic men, loving the masses and rather than killing them since we understood that they were being used, we held our fire. However, the leadership of the counter-revolutionary elements, headed by Maurice Bishop, Unison Whiteman and Vincent Noel, knowing that we did not want to harm the people disarmed the Officers and Chiefs and soldiers and began arming people who represented their own minority class interest.

Comrades, these men who preached for us that they had the interests of the Grenadian people at heart did not have one member of the working class controlling their criminal operations. These elements although they used the working class and working people to gain their objective did not have any confidence in them, and therefore had only businessmen, nuns, nurses and lumpen elements in the operations centre.

The presence of the people shows as clearly where they were coming from. Besides, Maurice Bishop, certain that they had won pointed out to the Officers that he did not want to have socialism built in this country.

These counter-revolutionaries who had given the assurance to the party before to resolve the crisis peacefully — were on the one hand trying to give assurance to the unarmed soldiers that nothing would happen while on the other hand they were preparing to murder all Party comrades, Officers and Chiefs that they held. Again this truth was borne out when Maurice Bishop openly stated that he was going to build a new Party and a new Army — to defend the interests of the bourgeoisie.

However, because of the prompt action of the reserve Force, guided by the Central Committee of the NJM — these dismayers of the masses were crushed. The timely move of our Motorized Units dealt a devastating blow to these criminals, those opportunist elements who did not want to see socialism built in our country and who were not interested in seeing the masses benefit more and more.

Comrades, today, Wednesday 19 October, history was made again. All patriots and revolutionaries will never forget this day when counter-revolution, the friends of imperialism were crushed. This victory today will ensure that our glorious Party, the NJM will live on and grow from strength to strength, leading and guiding the Armed Forces and the Revolution.

This victory is for progress and for socialism. But in giving this victory, one of our soldiers, Sgt. Byron Cameron, was wounded, while O.Cadet Conrad Mayers, WO.2 Raphael Dawson, Sgt. Dorset Peters and L'Cpl. Martin Simon died a hero's death.

Let our comrades' death be an inspiration to us, let it be a sign of the staunchness of our revolutionary Armed Forced and let us use it to strengthen our resolve to defend the Revolution and to build socialism.

Let this moment be proof to counter-revolution of our firmness, discipline and staunchness to the Party, the NJM, the working class, working people and to socialism. Let this be testimony of our unity behind our Party and Revolution.

We have won a victory comrades, but let us stand and be united to ensure that we achieve other victories.

LONG LIVE OUR PARTY, THE NJM!!
LONG LIVE THE PEOPLE'S REVOLUTIONARY ARMED
   FORCES!!
LONG LIVE THE GRENADA REVOLUTION!!
FORWARD EVER!! BACKWARD NEVER!!
SOCIALISM OR DEATH!!!

beginning of a partial and opportunist 'rehabilitation' of Maurice Bishop and an effective declaration of war on his successors. From the moment that the US ships changed course the possibility of an invasion became a probability. Although the RMC had put the island into quarantine and expelled foreign journalists, telephone and telex links with the outside world remained open and allowed the State Department and US intelligence services to construct a picture of what was occurring. Radio hams from the medical school also broadcast their version of events. Two of these — Jim Pfister and Mark B. Barettella — made a number of apparently coded transmissions and were later suspected of being agents of the CIA. Whatever the case, as Vice-Admiral Joseph Metcalf's force steamed towards the island Washington was evidently in a position to decide whether to invade.

After the event there was much conjecture as to how long before 25 October this decision was taken. Apart from a little publicised 'slip of the tongue' made on 26 October by Evan Galbraith, US ambassador to France, that the operation was 'an action which had begun two weeks ago', there is little hard evidence that a political decision was taken before Bishop's assassination. It was later confirmed that between 23 September and 2 October the 2nd Battalion of the 75th Rangers Division was practising the capture of an airport and freeing of hostages at Ephrata Municipal Airport, Washington state.

According to local authorities this exercise had been undertaken only once before, in 1981. However, the timing of this manoeuvre might be less critical than it appears since it is inconceivable that an operation on the scale of 'Urgent Fury' could be put into practice without considerable logistical preparation, which, as we have seen, had been under way since 1981. The principal issue facing the Reagan administration was less military organisation than the political means by which an invasion might be arranged and justified.

Friday 21 October proved to be a critical day in terms of preparing the offensive against the RMC. Affairs were concentrated in Bridgetown, Barbados, the seat of the US ambassador to the Eastern Caribbean, Milan Bish. On the 15th a member of Bish's staff had approached Tom Adams, the prime minister of Barbados, to sound him out about the possibility of 'rescuing' Maurice Bishop; the idea eventually came to nought. Six days later Barbados hosted a meeting of the states of the OECS, which has its headquarters in St Lucia and does not include Barbados. Grenada was not represented at this meeting. After considerable discussion and the voicing of doubts on the part of Antigua, the meeting decided to ask Washington for a military intervention in Grenada. The legal status of such a request is highly questionable (see box).

It also remains unclear whether the OECS acted on its own initiative or, as has been widely claimed, was responding to suggestions emanating from Washington. On the same day Adams, who was not entitled to attend the meeting, told the British high commissioner that the OECS was 'contemplating' asking the US to intervene. As a result, the British embassy in Washington asked the State Department to be kept fully informed of developments. Two days later — Sunday 23 October — Eugenia Charles, chairwoman of the OECS, sent a formal letter to Bish requesting action. This letter was received in Washington the same day. According to the Foreign Office, at no stage before the invasion did the British government or any of its embassies receive any written appeal or indication that the invasion was being prepared.

Even in Barbados itself knowledge of the OECS move was restricted to very few people. George Chambers, prime minister of Trinidad and Tobago, later complained bitterly to his colleagues in Caricom that he had chaired a meeting of Caricom in Bridgetown on 22 and 23 October completely unaware of this critical initiative being taken by a section of the organisation's member-states. Chamber's objections were particularly important since at its meeting Caricom rejected the idea of military intervention. In the debate Trinidad, Guyana, Belize and the Bahamas opposed a resolution in favour of an invasion that was backed most strongly by Barbados and Jamaica, which later

The Invasion of the Rule of Law

According to the Reagan administration, one of the principal objectives of its invasion of the state of Grenada was 'to restore order and democracy'. To back this up the US government stated that it had received a request for action from the Queen's Governor General on the island, Sir Paul Scoon, and the Organization of Eastern Caribbean States (OECS). Within hours of the operation the terms of such 'requests' came under considerable scrutiny, and the official US rendition of events appeared to be highly questionable. It was, for instance, evident that Scoon had made no written request for an invasion before he was safely on board the US warship Guam; that is, after the invasion was actually taking place. Equally, several well-placed sources contended that the OECS request was drafted by officials in Washington and simply relayed back to its authors from the Caribbean. Leaving aside these important doubts as well as the equally important factor, raised by Arthur Schlesinger in the *Wall Street Journal,* that the invasion 'would have a little more plausibility if we showed an equal determination to restore order and democracy in, say, Haiti or Chile', the invasion still represented an open violation of international law. A number of prominent US lawyers drew attention to this fact and discussed some of its historical precedents in the press (see Appendix 4), but it requires little specialist knowledge to perceive that a number of international accords were broken.

The UN Charter states, 'all nations shall refrain in their international relations from threat or use of force against the territorial integrity or political independence of any state'. Armed force may be used when sanctioned by the UN, but the OECS in no sense constitutes a substitute for the UN.

The Organisation of American States (OAS) Charter states, Chapter IV, Article 14, that, 'the right of a state to protect and develop its existence does not authorize it to execute unjust acts against another state'.

Article 18 of the OAS Charter states, 'No state or group of states has the right to intervene, directly or indirectly, for any reason whatever, in the internal or external affairs of any other state', whether by armed force or any other means.

Article 20 of the same charter, signed by Grenada and all the states who invaded her, states: 'The territory of a state is inviolable; it may not be the object, even temporarily, of military occupation or other measures of force taken by another state, directly or indirectly, on any grounds whatever.'

In the US government's first official publication on the invasion, *Grenada: A Preliminary Report,* the State Department declares that the military intervention had a 'firm legal foundation'. This was, in part, because Washington undertook operations in response 'to a formal request for assistance from the Organisation of Eastern Caribbean States (OECS), a regional grouping of Dominica, St. Lucia, Montserrat, St Christopher-Nevis, Antigua and Barbuda, St Vincent and the Grenadines, and Grenada. At a meeting held in Bridgetown, Barbados, on 21 October, these democratic countries determined by unanimous vote that conditions in Grenada required action under the 1981 treaty that established the OECS.' This official statement does not reveal that the OECS request was made under Article 8 of the 1981 treaty, which concerns itself not with inter-island disputes or affairs but 'arrangements for collective security against external aggression'. Moreover, this article states unequivocally that any decision made under it 'shall be unanimous'. In this respect the wording of the US statement needs to be scrutinised closely for such a decision was not made unanimously; Grenada was not represented.

joined with the OECS and the US in sending troops to Grenada. The final Caricom decision was to impose trade and diplomatic sanctions on the RMC. Although this appears to be a somewhat weak move, such measures would have brought the Grenadian economy to a halt very rapidly because the island lacked proper oil storage facilities and large supplies of essential goods. However great the advances made by the PRG in the economic field, the island still remained dependent upon a high level of co-operation from its larger and richer neighbours. Bishop's ability to obtain Trinidad's support within Caricom had forestalled the possibility of a blockade in the past, but now such a link had disappeared.

The probability of a blockade and the growing possibility of an invasion were perceived within hours of Bishop's death inside Grenada and in the rest of the Caribbean. Following his strong condemnation of the assassination, Fidel Castro instructed the 784 Cuban personnel on the island to remain, but he also tried to open discussions with Washington in order to avert further chaos and bloodshed. A message to this effect was sent to the US interests section of the Swiss embassy in Havana on Sunday 23 October. As Castro later explained in an exceptionally detailed and forceful speech, Cuban relations with the RMC were very cold indeed, but Havana perceived a need to desist from intervening in the internal disputes of the Grenadian party, above all at a time when external intervention was threatened (see Appendix 3). Soviet public pronouncements on the establishment of the RMC were markedly warmer than those issued by Cuba and even prompted some commentators to suggest a major split had occurred over the issue.

Within three days of military rule being imposed in Grenada there were a number of signs that the RMC itself had begun to appreciate the consequences of the events of the 19th. The curfew was maintained throughout the weekend of 22-23 October and the armed forces put on alert for an invasion. However, on Saturday 22nd Austin drew up a statement declaring that the RMC was to be a strictly temporary government, that a civilian administration was to be appointed within 12 days, and that a team would be appointed to investigate the events of the 19th. This statement was transmitted to Washington and London over the weekend, although neither government admitted receiving it until after the invasion, and doubts were cast on the RMC's intentions of putting its declaration into practice. Nonetheless, officials from the medical school who spoke to Austin over the weekend reported that he emphasised the necessity of a return to some form of constitutional government. Moreover, it is possible that once the officers of the PRA perceived external developments and had been brought face to face with the depth of popular sentiment within the island, some of them at least contemplated making a retreat. Austin himself had never been a committed member of Coard's group and lacked strong political convictions; his subordinates Layne and James had been the prime movers of a more resolute imposition of party discipline within the government and the army. Equally, it is possible that Bernard Coard himself finally came to appreciate the severity of the situation and opted for a change of direction in the hope that an invasion might be averted. The fact that the declaration of the 22nd was drawn up at all suggests that a debate was taking place inside the new regime, some members of which at least had decided not to pursue any further the course of militarism and party diktat imposed from 13 October onwards. It was the stated aim of Caricom to put on pressure precisely to hasten such a change without making recourse to military activity. In view of the fact that over the weekend Austin agreed to meet the premier of St. Lucia, John Compton, the possibility of such a strategy succeeding cannot be ruled out. From midday on Saturday 22 October, all the signals emanating from Grenada pointed to a growing disposition to negotiate.

The clearest sign that this was the case related to the treatment of the 600 US medical students on the island. According to the State Department document published six weeks after the invasion, 'in exchanges with visiting US officials on 23 and 24 October, senior People's Revolutionary Army officers repeatedly raised impediments to the orderly evacuation of US citizens desiring to leave the island.' Such a version does not tally at all with the account given by the school's vice-chancellor, who personally handled relations with the

RMC (see box). According to the State Department, which fails to mention that the RMC facilitated the visit of its officials, these functionaries 'concluded that American *(sic)* lives were in jeopardy and that a peaceful, orderly evacuation would not be possible'. On Monday 24 October, the Barbadian press quoted one of the returning US officials, Kenneth Kurze, as saying of the students, 'we have not recommended to them that they leave'. Given that Barbados and the OECS governments, now co-operating closely with the US, refused to allow the local airline, LIAT, to fly to Grenada to evacuate foreign nationals at this juncture, such a statement might be seen less as a confirmation of the students' safety than as part of a deliberate plan to keep them on the island and thereby provide the US with a justification for invading. Some British and Canadian citizens as well as a small number of US students did leave on the 23rd in chartered aircraft, which were in no way impeded from flying by the Grenadian authorities. Thus, those US citizens who wanted to leave were allowed to; most did not and, in contrast to the case of British nationals, were not encouraged to either by the advice of their government or by the carefully organised lack of sufficient aircraft. In view of the fact that 'Ocean Venture 81' had been organised around a supposed liberation of hostages and since memories of the humiliation suffered by the US over the hostages in Iran remained strong, such a course of action would seem logical if Washington was to provide itself with some humanitarian rationale for an invasion. Subsequent television pictures of a number of US students gratefully kissing the ground on their return to the US greatly helped to reinforce this image of the operation. At the time no commentator made reference to the fact that these young people had been obliged, as a result of State Department advice, to endure two days of heavy gunfire and to suffer an extraordinarily dangerous evacuation.

The departure of the State Department officials on the 23rd without the great majority of the US students appears to mark an irreversible decision on the part of the Reagan administration to pursue the option of an invasion. Such a decision must also have been hardened by the news that on that day 230 US marines had been killed by a bomb that destroyed their barracks in Beirut, where they were acting as part of a 'peace-keeping' force. The difficulties and losses suffered by the US contingent in Beirut had already led to much domestic criticism of the Reagan government, which seemed to have committed itself to a militarily hopeless and politically damaging operation. Although the US action in Lebanon had been supported by France, Italy and Great Britain, it was viewed by many abroad as little less than a unilateral move and a further indication of the administration's tendency to marginalise the UN, about which some senior US officials, including

The Protection of Life and Limb

As with most modern military operations, 'Urgent Fury' involved careful management of the news media. In addition to excluding the press from the island until US troops were clearly in command — an exclusion that was presented as protecting the safety of correspondents — such management entailed extensive disinformation and misinformation. Such terms can, in some cases, be the equivalent of what is known in plain English as 'lying'. President Reagan was centrally involved in the presentation of the US government's version of events and rationale for invading. At the press conference given early on 25 October in the company of Eugenia Charles, prime minister of Dominica, the US president cited three basic reasons for violating Grenada's territorial integrity: 'to assist in the restoration of conditions of order and democracy'; to forestall 'further chaos'; and, first of all, to protect the lives of some 1,000 US citizens, including 600 students at St George's University medical school. It will be remembered that the 'Ocean Venture 81' manoeuvres were organised around a supposed kidnapping of US citizens.

Following the events of 19 October the US government laid constant stress on the danger faced by the students, fee-paying pupils who had failed to gain admission to US medical schools. The existence of such a danger was placed in considerable doubt by an article in the *Los Angeles Times* (6 November 1983) written by Peter G. Bourne, the son of the school's vice-chancellor and himself a visiting professor there:

'Concerned for my father's safety and that of the other faculty members and students at the school, I contacted my father who assured me not only that there was no cause for alarm, but that Coard had guaranteed the safety of the medical school and students. We remained in contact over the next several days by telephone and through the medical school telex link to its Bayshore office in New York. After Bishop's murder, my father continued to feel that the safety of the students was assured. Despite a 24-hour curfew, Coard provided government vehicles so that students could get from one campus to another in safety.

'On Wednesday 19 October, I received a call from a member of the board of trustees, a distinguished and conservative man who said that the State Department was pressuring school officials in New York to say publicly that the students in Grenada were in danger so that Washington would have a pretext to invade the island. I urged that they not accede to such pressure.

'Meanwhile on Grenada, my father was continuing to hold discussions initially with Coard and subsequently with General Hudson Austin, the head of the new military council. Austin expressed his strong desire that the medical school remain on the island and promised to guarantee the safety of the students. He provided my father with his home phone number and said that if my father had any concern about the students' safety to call him at any hour of the day or night . . . Still concerned about the safety of the medical students in the event of a US invasion, my father convinced Austin to allow representatives of the US embassy in Barbados to come to the island the next morning, Saturday 22 October. Austin agreed, and the message was relayed to the State Department via the medical school office in New York.

'US embassy officials met with Austin and other members of the military council and the medical students. It was my father's hope that once these officials realized that the students and faculty were in no danger and had also a chance to see the political direction in which Austin wanted to move that it would be clear an invasion was entirely unwarranted.

'That night the bombing in Beirut occurred. My father felt that an invasion of Grenada was thus unlikely. Nevertheless, he convened a meeting of the students and said that anyone who wished to leave could do so. About 10 per cent expressed such a desire, mainly first-semester students who had been in Grenada only six weeks.

'On Monday morning the airport was reopened as General Austin had promised, and any students who wanted to leave could do so. The only problem was that Barbados was already preparing with Washington to invade the next day and refused to let the commercial airline LIAT fly to the island. A few students left by charter plane as did British and Canadian citizens alarmed by the continuing rumours of imminent invasion.

'That same morning I received a telegram from my father, who apparently felt he would not be able to communicate with me in any other way, which said, "We are all still well and safe. News distorted and exaggerated." However, in the early afternoon, (Charles) Modica (the school's chancellor) called me to say that he had talked by phone with my father who felt increasingly that Austin wanted to move the country back toward democracy. He was seeking guidance and help from my father, who asked that I draft a strategy paper to help Austin accomplish such a transition. The paper was written in Washington that afternoon. I transmitted it to New York and at 11 that night it was read to my father over the telephone. Because there was no apparent urgency, it was agreed that the paper would be telexed in its entirety the next morning.

'The invasion began six hours later.'

One of the greatest ironies of the management of the students' safety was that the majority were finally evacuated under conditions that were far more dangerous than those prevailing before the invasion. On the afternoon of Wednesday 26 October, US troops ferried most of the students to a beach on Grand Anse Bay, where fighting was still taking place. As the first helicopters approached to lift the US citizens off they attracted heavy fire from the hills overlooking the bay and had to take rapid and dangerous evasive action. Subsequent and sustained air-raids on the hill area wiped out the PRA detachment stationed there and no students were seriously injured, but the final 'rescue operation' — the term adopted by Ronald Reagan to describe this entire historic episode — was a distinctly foolhardy and unprofessional undertaking.

Ambassador Jeane Kirkpatrick, had recently made disparaging comments. The setback suffered in Beirut promised to increase domestic and foreign criticism and reflected badly on US military prowess. The operation planned for Grenada offered a chance to restore Washington's reputation as a world power, provide substance for the administration's claims that it was combating the 'Soviet-Cuban conspiracy', and destroy a troublesome regime in the name of protecting innocent lives and restoring democracy. Moreover, the situation inside Grenada appeared to be excellent for staging such a 'rescue mission'. These factors outweighed fears of the illegality of an invasion.

Such apprehension certainly existed in some circles in Washington that had not forgotten the recent experience of the Argentine invasion of the Falklands, over which the US had supported Britain. Yet, although the US borrowed many military lessons from the British campaign and emulated its strict control of press coverage, it chose both to ignore the legal aspect and not to liaise closely with London over Grenada. This caused the Thatcher government considerable embarrassment since the island was formerly a British colony and a member of the Commonwealth with a government presided over, in name at least, by the Queen's governor general, Sir Paul Scoon. There is still much doubt over Scoon's role in the days immediately prior to the invasion as well as some confusion as to the nature of the information imparted to the Foreign Office by the State Department. The version provided by Reagan and Eugenia Charles at their press conference of the morning of the 25th was that Scoon had asked the OECS for outside help. This request was also said to have been made in a letter, but there is no evidence to substantiate any claim that the governor general wrote a letter until he was aboard a US warship, two days after the invasion had been undertaken. It is possible that Scoon was unable to make such a request despite the fact that the RMC continued to recognise him as the Queen's representative and governor general of the island. He was certainly able to make telephone calls abroad over the weekend of 22-23 October. On the 22nd Buckingham Palace phoned him to enquire after his health and position; he made no appeal for help to the only authority to which he was legally answerable. The next day Scoon had a long telephone conversation with the Commonwealth Secretariat, informed them that the RMC had expressed a desire to hand over to a civilian government and discussed the possibility of an international investigation being made into the events of the 19th; again, however, the governor general made no appeal for help. On the Monday Scoon was able to have an interview with Brigadier Rudy Lewis of the Barbadian armed forces. It is stated that at this meeting he did ask for help but said that an invasion was the last thing he wanted. In view of this evidence, it is possible to understand not only why there was considerable scepticism over the nature of the alleged 'requests' made by the governor general but also why the British government remained ignorant of developments until the last moment. As a result, Foreign Secretary Sir Geoffrey Howe's declaration to the Commons as late as 4pm on the 24th that the government knew of no intention to invade, and Mrs Thatcher's subsequent efforts to dissuade President Reagan from taking such a course, appeared both unconvincing and indicative of a lack of authority and influence. It is possible that the British government believed the statements of Reagan's press secretary, Larry Speakes, who declared on the 24th that the US fleet was in the vicinity of Grenada to 'monitor' the situation, that there were 'no plans for US military action in Grenada', and that rumours of an invasion were 'preposterous'.

In Grenada, Monday 24 October was marked by contradictory developments. On the one hand, the RMC continued to mobilise the PRA in readiness for an armed incursion. On the other, the curfew was lifted and people encouraged to return to work. The response was mixed. Apart from a brief break on Friday between 10am and 2pm — to permit the purchase of essential items — the population had been inside for four days with the radio repeating news of the arrival of the US fleet and issuing instructions in preparation for an invasion. Amid considerable tension an estimated 70 per cent of the labour force returned to work. However, the RMC correctly considered that much of the militia was opposed to the government and therefore held back from a general distribution of arms. Although some young members of the militia and the NYO did rally to the call, the absence of a general mobilisation and the deep suspicion on both sides reflected the complete division of the NJM from the mass of Grenadians. On the next day the 600 members of the PRA were left to fight with minimal popular assistance.

5 Invasion

Urgent Fury

President Reagan referred to the invasion of 25 October as a military operation conducted with 'surgical precision'. In fact, it was nothing of the sort. Despite possessing enormous advantages in every respect except surprise Admiral Metcalf's taskforce displayed a notable lack of intelligence and tactical skill. As a result, the US armed forces put themselves, the US citizens on the island and the Grenadian civilian population at great risk. They also proved to be exceedingly slow in liquidating resistance from a force a tenth of their size operating, without air support, heavy weapons and any significant popular backing in an island only 20 miles long.

The invasion, code-named 'Urgent Fury', was declared to be a joint operation between contingents from the OECS states, the US, Jamaica and Barbados, which was the starting point for the airborne landings. However, the initial force of 1,900 marines which landed early on the 25th was composed entirely of US troops. More than 4,000 troops called in as reinforcements over the following two days as the invasion encountered unexpected obstacles were also from the US, as were the further 10,000 men aboard the taskforce ships. The initial Caribbean contingent of 300 men, 150 of whom came from Jamaica, did not engage in any fighting and were only deployed on police duty once combat had ceased. These men acted directly under US orders. To all intents and purposes the invasion was planned and executed by the US. Its allies merely provided a token presence and public statements of support.

The first group of soldiers to land on the island early on the 25th was a squadron of naval commandos who made their way to the governor general's residence in an effort to extract Sir Paul Scoon. This elite group managed to reach the house but was then surprised by the PRA. The exchange of fire that followed could not have alleviated Sir Paul's concern for his own safety; it was two days before he was evacuated to a US warship. By 5.40am large numbers of marines had landed at Pearls and Point Salines airports. At Pearls there was no resistance and a bridgehead was established immediately. At Point Salines the US troops surprised Cuban construction workers and a prolonged but intermittent exchange of fire ensued. According to President Castro the Cubans were under orders to defend themselves if attacked but not to fire first. The testimonies of Cuban construction workers involved in this incident are unanimous in their assertion that the marines initiated hostilities. They also refer to the use of captured Cubans as a human shield behind which the US troops advanced on remaining pockets of resistance (see Appendix 3). A second group of Cubans, who had received military training, as do all adult citizens of that country, refused to surrender and was attacked on the following day even though the US government was aware of the orders that had been issued to them. In all, some 24 Cuban personnel were killed and 59 wounded on 25 and 26 October; the proportion of dead to wounded was abnormally high for what might be termed 'ordinary' combat conditions.

Despite having overcome Cuban resistance in the vicinity of Point Salines on the Tuesday, the US forces did not declare the airport safe until the Thursday. This was partly because opposition from the PRA proved to be more resolute than was anticipated. However, the delay in US advances on the ground may also be attributed to the high number of accidents and casualties they inflicted upon themselves, the disorientation of many marines — some of whom were equipped with tourist maps and did not know several days after the landing whether the PRA was on their side or not — and a disposition to rely upon airpower. The bombing raids made on Tuesday and Wednesday and throughout the nights destroyed much civilian property and sowed a sense of panic amongst the population. It was in such a raid that the Richmond Hill mental hospital was destroyed, killing over 30 patients.

It was only after three days, the landing of 6,000 troops, numerous sorties by aircraft, and the evacuation of a large part of the population of the south of the island to St George's that US troops occupied the capital. Shortly thereafter the Pentagon issued statements that had been prepared for dissemination on the Tuesday. As members of the

PRA began to surrender, the population of the capital emerged to offer thanks for the ending of a fortnight of extreme apprehension. The US media were finally permitted to enter the island in order to relay this to the outside world.

The exclusion of the press from the island until it had been secured by the invasion force gave the US military a free hand to impose its version of events. A small number of foreign journalists had managed to reach the island by a circuitous route shortly before the landing. Yet although they filed early reports that challenged the official US account of the numbers and activity of the Cubans on Grenada, the numbers of casualties on all sides, the nature of the final evacuation of the students, and the existence of remaining pockets of resistance, Washington's word continued to carry great weight. The normally curious and investigative US press corps was obliged to wait in Barbados and relay official statements.

Having declared that Grenada was a 'Soviet-Cuban colony being readied as a major military bastion to export terror and undermine democracy', President Reagan intimated that Cuba was behind the events of 19 October, that Cuban troops had provided the bulk of the opposition to the invasion, and that they continued to be engaged in military operations even after the fall of St George's. Two days after the landing the US government stated that there were at least 1,100 and maybe up to 2,000 Cubans on the island, that all were trained soldiers and most were 'impersonating' construction workers. As late as the 28th Admiral Metcalf stated that 'several hundred Cubans had escaped into Grenada's hills and could cause problems for US troops in the coming weeks' (*Washington Post,* 30 October 1983). On 30 October the Cuban government declared that there were precisely 784 of its nationals on the island, less than 30 of whom were military advisers. In response Metcalf stated, 'That's patently false. If you believe that, we've already killed and captured more people than they have here.' The State Department later confirmed the Cuban figures after Havana listed the name, age, profession, employer and home town of all its citizens in Grenada. This list showed that the great majority were far too old to be on active military service and that the US forces had already killed or captured all the Cubans on Grenada. Nonetheless, the US military persisted in referring to the existence of Cubans 'in the mountains' for a number of days afterwards.

Similar confusion surrounded US declarations during the week of the invasion that there were 30 Soviet and an undisclosed number of East German military advisers on the island. None was subsequently produced. Equally, President Reagan's statement that his forces had discovered warehouses 'stacked to the ceiling' with weapons and ammunition, 'enough to supply thousands of terrorists', had a considerable impact and appeared to justify claims that Grenada had become a military stronghold. However, further inspection and calculation revealed that the warehouses were only half-full, and instead of containing sufficient weapons to arm a '14,000 to 17,000-man expeditionary force', there were 6,323 rifles, only 800 of which were 'reasonably modern' and many of which were antiques from the nineteenth century.

Official US statements with respect to casualty figures also manifested a degree of flexibility that troubled the foreign press. This was partly because numbers of US casualties resulting from 'friendly fire' were not counted as being incurred in combat, partly because of the manifest exaggeration of the number of Cubans, and also because the US military displayed a marked reluctance to assess the scale of Grenadian casualties, both military and civilian. For over a week no serious effort was made by the invasion force to locate, count or bury the bodies of local people. In a typical incident, an Irish priest, Father Sean Doggett, discovered the bodies of three young militiamen who had died defending the RFG transmission station and been left to rot in the building for six days. Having dug a grave but finding no protective clothing with which to make the burial, Father Duggett approached a US colonel for assistance. The officer replied that he and his men had come to kill the enemy, not to bury them. Such a response meant that a great many bodies were finally interred by the civilian population after they had been located by smell. Even after the US forces had taken the trouble to count every bullet they had captured — 5,615,682 — they were unable to say how many Grenadians had been killed or wounded. According to Mr Speakes, this was because Grenadians had a religious custom of immediately burying their dead; this statement was later withdrawn when the White House was informed that the majority of the islanders were Roman Catholic. At the end of the year the State Department announced that US casualties totalled 18 dead and 116 wounded in action, and that 45 Grenadians were killed and 337 wounded. These figures were not immediately ratified by local sources, some of which remarked upon the cursory manner in which the US forces searched the rubble of Richmond Hill hospital before having it bulldozed in.

Within two days of landing officials of military psychological operations ('PSYOPS') teams and the CIA had not only herded most of the Cubans into a controlled area at Point Salines but also rounded up hundreds of Grenadians. These people were treated uniformly as captives despite the fact that many of them, such as George Louison, had opposed the RMC and been detained under its rule. The treatment of the detained Grenadians did not even conform to that given to prisoners of war — they were locked into small packing cases standing in a sweltering heat for long periods, a practice in direct contravention of the Geneva Convention. After a preliminary round of interrogation, important prisoners, such as Bernard and Phyllis Coard and Hudson Austin, were taken to US ships for further questioning. Their precise status as prisoners and the legal basis for their extradition were never declared although the US military declared that they had been taken off the island 'for their own safety'. Some days later they were returned to Grenada. Shortly thereafter the island was plastered with posters of Bernard Coard photographed in a style reminiscent of the Vietnam war: blindfolded, handcuffed and dressed only in pyjama trousers. Three months after the invasion 32 prisoners, including all the members of the RMC, were being held without charge, raising a number of important legal and constitutional problems for the new interim government. However, in the aftermath of the landing the US forces did occasionally concern themselves, albeit on very dubious grounds, with the fine points of protocol. It was later discovered that 27 US military policemen had sworn an oath of allegiance to Queen Elizabeth in order to serve under the Grenadian commissioner of police and thus have legal authority to arrest and detain Grenadians.

For a week after the invasion there were isolated incidents of sniper fire, but as the US forces combed the inland hills, tightened up road blocks, made extensive house-to-house searches, and drafted in more Caribbean troops and police, resistance petered out. By the end of October the bulk of the PRA had surrendered, PSYOPS teams had covered the island with their propaganda and were ready to transmit over 'Spice Island Radio' which had replaced RFG, and a 50-strong group of State Department officials under Deputy Assistant Secretary of State Charles Gillespie had established the first US diplomatic mission on the island and was effectively running civil administration from the Ross Point Inn. The CIA had also completed initial interrogation of 'suspects' detained by US forces with the active assistance of ex-members of the Mongoose Gang recently released from jail as well as other opponents of the NJM. It was clear that the invasion had been accomplished successfully. Sir Paul Scoon declared, 'The Americans have done a bloody good job'. While most Grenadians would not, perhaps, have employed such an unfortunate form of words, they were undoubtedly pleased at the outcome of events and, most important of all, grateful that revenge had been exacted for the murder of Maurice Bishop. It was not so obvious whether they appreciated the international consequences of the invasion or the local ramifications of occupation by foreign soldiers. For the first few weeks such matters were clearly not uppermost in the mind of ordinary Grenadians.

The Aftermath Abroad

Immediately following the landing of US troops in Grenada public opinion within the US was divided over the wisdom and morality of the invasion. On 26 October, the editors of the *Washington Post* called it an 'immensely grave act', expressed concern over the legal justifications presented by the administration, and were particularly worried by the deaths of the Cubans:

The United States has killed some Cubans and captured others, all people who were in Grenada by official invitation. It will not do to say that some were shot at because they refused to lay down their arms. It is an extremely serious business to violate the lives and liberties of Third Country nationals. To . . . seek military information from some of the captives compounds the violation.

However, the grateful response of the Grenadian people, the rescue of the students, and the backing given by the majority of English-speaking countries in the Caribbean helped to build up support for the administration. The military success of the operation at a relatively low cost of (US) lives was also important in this respect. From the evidence of opinion polls, many citizens of the US shared the view of an army sergeant interviewed in St. George's after the invasion: 'We're here to stop the Cubans oppressing the Grenadians. It's not an excuse, it's a damned good reason.' In the wake of Beirut a victorious little war that dealt a sharp blow to the forces at odds with the US had great appeal for the *Wall Street Journal,* a paper that had recently begun to increase its criticism of the administration's economic and foreign policies. According to the issue of the *Journal* published on 28 October, the lesson of the invasion of Grenada,

is that, when necessary and appropriate, the US can and should rely on its military power to achieve its political goals . . . the lesson is that it's once again known that the US is *willing to use its military as an instrument of policy.*

Popular support for such a view and widespread acceptance of Reagan's use of the term 'rescue mission' had the effect of curbing congressional disquiet and sustaining the administration's efforts to establish a 'bipartisan' approach to Central America and the Caribbean. Nevertheless, a week after the invasion the Democratic majority in the House of Representatives called for a withdrawal of troops within 60 days. This was principally an endeavour to halt what was perceived as the government's increasingly flamboyant disregard for the War Powers Act and its propensity for engaging in military activity without congressional approval. However, the measure also reflected extreme concern on Capitol Hill over the almost unanimous international opposition to the invasion.

The British response was most widely commented upon since London had attempted and failed to forestall the invasion. On the 26th the Conservative government refused a call from the Labour Party opposition to condemn the operation, but Mrs Thatcher did not hide from the Commons the fact that she had told Reagan of her 'considerable doubts' over the plan. In response, Denis Healey, the shadow foreign secretary, accused the prime minister of being Reagan's 'poodle' and Sir Geoffrey Howe of demonstrating 'pitiable impotence, quite unworthy of a British Foreign Secretary'. While the State Department confessed to a 'deep sense of outrage' at Britain's lack of support, even conservative opinion in Britain was rallying against Washington's operation. On 26 October the editors of the *Times* began their leader:

There is no getting away from the fact that the United States and its Caribbean allies have committed an act of aggression against Grenada. They are in breach of international law and the Charter of the United Nations. None of (President Reagan's) reasons provides legal justification for an attack on an independent state.

Statements such as these were so clearly linked to the experience of the Falklands war that five days after the invasion the British prime minister, for whose domestic popularity the war had been extremely important, was obliged to stiffen her response by stating that, 'the West cannot just walk into other countries'. Such a strong declaration by one of Washington's otherwise most assiduous supporters also reflected the damage the invasion had on the Conservative government's campaign to persuade the British public of the co-operative and peaceable nature of its Atlantic ally at a time when the debate over nuclear weapons had become a key political issue as a result of the arrival of US cruise missiles in Europe. Other European and NATO governments, equally concerned by this issue and the Reagan administration's penchant for unilateral military activity, were also highly critical. The conservative Kohl government in West Germany complained that it had only been informed of the operation by the US ambassador in Bonn six hours after the landings took place; Foreign Minister Genscher then proceeded to make a strenuous reiteration of the principle of non-interference. French President Mitterand likened the operation to the Soviet invasion of Afghanistan and the Libyan invasion of Chad; even the government of Japan called the use of force 'regrettable'.

The definition of the invasion by the Soviet news agency Tass as 'a crime against peace and humanity' was perhaps predictable, but China's condemnation of it as 'naked, bloody aggression' represented a major setback for the State Department's policy of continued rapprochement with Peking. The response of the OAS was scarcely less critical. At a meeting held two days after the invasion only four OECS states attempted to support the invasion and even the Dominican Republic, which had been occupied by US troops in 1965, called it 'deplorable'. The attitude of many normally pro-US governments was summed up by the chairman of the Permanent Council of the OAS, Bolivian ambassador Fernando Salazar Paredes:

Any intervention, regardless of the motives, would constitute a violation of the charter (of the OAS) . . . This is Grenada; it could be any country tomorrow. It reminds us a little bit of the Dominican Republic.

Aside from the OECS and Israel, only the governments of El Salvador, Chile, Guatemala and Uruguay expressed support for the intervention in the UN; none of these regimes had produced any evidence of supporting the 'restoration of democracy' in their own countries. The resolution of condemnation presented to the UN was sponsored by Nicaragua, Guyana and Zimbabwe. The US veto meant that this resolution stood no chance of success in the Security Council, but in the General Assembly it received overwhelming support. In the final vote on 3 November, 108 countries condemned the invasion as a breach of the UN Charter and 9 supported it. The corresponding vote over the Soviet invasion of Afghanistan had been 104 against and 18 in favour.

Nicaragua's sponsorship of the motion of condemnation reflected the fears of the Sandinista government that their country was about to be invaded by US-backed forces from Honduras. In response, Reagan told a White House press conference, 'I haven't believed anything they've been saying since they got in charge and you shouldn't either'. The Nicaraguan fears did, however, appear to be very well-founded. Well before the invasion of Grenada the US had been conducting an extensive military 'exercise' off Nicaragua's shores and along its border with Honduras. This exercise, known as 'Big Pine Two', was planned to last at least until March 1984 and involved over 4,000 US ground forces. Amongst their manoeuvres were the building of roads from the Honduran interior to the border and the construction of new airstrips and military bases inside the country. Although some 10,000 counter-revolutionary troops (contras) of the pro-Somoza Frente Democratico Nicaraguense (FDN) were not formally included in these operations, it was an open secret that the US forces were collaborating closely with them. Moreover, the Reagan administration had budgeted over US$19 million for CIA 'covert' support for the contras and the US president publicly referred to them as 'freedom fighters'. In the first week of November the Republican majority in the US

Senate approved the Intelligence Authorization Bill which enabled US$19.9 million to be spent over the following six months to fund contra activity aimed at overthrowing the government of Nicaragua. Throughout 1983 there were 620 contra air actions over Nicaragua (compared with 275 in 1982), 400 of which came from Honduras. According to the FSLN government, there were 160 naval operations launched against its forces. Of these 60 involved violation of Nicaraguan territorial waters and 100 involved US vessels. In addition, contra guerilla groups had undertaken over 900 military operations, in 56 of which Honduran military collaboration was alleged. Throughout the year 346 civilians had been killed in military attacks. The Reagan government continued to call for more money to be given to the armed opposition even though it had been unable to provide proof of Nicaraguan military support for the guerillas in El Salvador for nearly three years.

The second week in November marked the peak of tension in Central America with air-raid shelters being dug in Nicaragua, the armed forces being placed on full alert, a number of foreigners leaving the country, and registration for obligatory military service being accelerated. The US citizens in Nicaragua pointedly sent a letter to their president declaring that under no circumstances did they wish to be 'rescued'.

One month previously the commanders and chiefs of staff of the armed forces of El Salvador, Guatemala, Honduras and Panama and the senior US officer from the Panama Canal Zone had attended a meeting in Guatemala City at which these generals decided to reform the Central American Defence Council (Condeca), which had been dormant since the 1969 war between Honduras and El Salvador. On 27 October, two days after US troops landed in Grenada, Adolfo Calero Portocarrero, a leader of the contra FDN, declared, 'There is an invasion plan for Nicaragua and it is supported by Condeca'. On 10 November, the *New York Times* reported that at a meeting of Condeca held in Tegucigalpa, capital of Honduras, representatives had recommended that their governments study whether 'legal instruments' might 'permit the security and armed forces of Panama and the other Central American countries to participate in action for the pacification of Nicaragua'. That week some 3,000 FDN and 2,000 Honduran troops were stationed on the Nicaraguan border.

The impact of the invasion in the Caribbean was little less emphatic. Having received such a strong impetus from Washington, Jamaica and Barbados, the strongest and most belligerent Caricom states involved in the intervention, launched diplomatic and political offensives at home and abroad. Barbadian premier Tom Adams ordered the expulsion of Rickey Singh, the Guyanese editor of the

Caribbean Council of Churches' paper, *Caribbean Contact*. Singh had worked in Barbados since 1974 and had consistently criticised the governments of Forbes Burnham in Guyana, which opposed the invasion, and that of Adams himself. After the paper came out strongly against the invasion, Singh was given 24 hours to leave Barbados. Adams also demanded that the Trinidadian ambassador to Bridgetown be withdrawn immediately; at the same time he sought US financial support for a Caribbean regional defence force. Following Reagan's tactic of posthumously praising Maurice Bishop so as to cover up previous deep-seated enmity to the PRG and to appear to have acted on a point of principle only when Bishop fell, Adams happily recounted the State Department's offer of 'rescuing' Bishop made to him on 15 October. According to the Barbadian premier, 'I concluded that, whatever our differences in the past, Mr Bishop deserved the support of the Caribbean countries'.

This avowed sentiment was not given much credit by the government of Trinidad, which had to some extent defended the PRG against the Caribbean 'hawks'. The attacks now made on the Chambers government by Barbados and the government of Edward Seaga in Jamaica represented not only resentment at the Trinidadian refusal to back the invasion but also revenge for Chamber's opposition to Seaga's efforts over the last two years to expel Grenada and Guyana from Caricom. This proposal took the form of a demand that the organisation make membership conditional upon respect for human rights and that decisions be binding according to majority rather than unanimous vote. According to Seaga, Grenada and Guyana habitually violated human rights, but in their place he wanted Caricom to include not only the Dominican Republic but also Haiti, the government of which certainly supported the US but equally certainly violated human rights on a scale comparable only with Somoza or the Shah of Iran. In the days following the invasion the press of Jamaica and Barbados made reference to 'traitors' in the Caribbean camp, and invective against Trinidad and Guyana was particularly fierce. Trinidad's oil wealth and economic importance for its neighbours appeared to safeguard the future of Caricom, but never had relations between its members been so poor. The traditional Commonwealth attachments of the English-speaking countries of the region were also placed in jeopardy by sharp criticism of London by the OECS, Jamaica and Barbados, and their explicit appeal to Washington to take over as economic prefect of the area. Seaga challenged the Commonwealth states to provide a 'peacekeeping' force to garrison Grenada and when they refused declared that the countries that had invaded would 'go it alone'. The Commonwealth summit at Delhi was the scene of sharp exchanges but in an effort to hold the organisation intact no vote was held.

The Jamaican government also took maximum political advantage from the invasion at home. Late in November, Seaga, a committed proponent of economic liberalism, devalued the Jamaican dollar by 43.5 per cent against the US dollar in order to meet IMF requirements for the payment of part of a US$650 million loan. Ex-prime minister Michael Manley, leader of the opposition People's National Party (PNP), immediately called for Seaga's resignation as minister of finance for weakening Jamaica's economic independence and sacrificing popular living standards on behalf of international capital. Seaga's response was not to resign but to make use of the temporary wave of popularity he was enjoying as a result of Jamaica's prominent role in the Grenada operation and call a general election for 15 December. Since this allowed the opposition only three weeks to organise for a poll two months before scheduled elections and on the basis of an old voters' register which was estimated to omit some 250,000 voters, most of whom were young and thought to oppose Seaga, the PNP decided to boycott the election. As a result, Seaga returned virtually unopposed for another term of office at a time of economic crisis. Jamaica's already unsteady parliamentary system was further weakened by an effective opposition being absent from the legislature and the prospect of a return to political violence. The first indications of this occurred even before Seaga's 'constitutional coup' when a demonstration against the invasion was repressed with great violence by the police. The principal victim in this instance was the pro-Moscow Workers Party of Jamaica (WPJ), led by Trevor Munroe, who had actively supported the central committee of the NJM against Bishop.

The WPJ now became the object of concerted government harrassment and, like the rest of the left in the region, was badly damaged both by the internal collapse of the Grenadian revolution and the reactionary backlash that followed it. The small island parties that had looked to the NJM for leadership and saw Grenada as a symbol of the future were obliged to take a very low profile and reassess their policies. Almost all of these groups had, with greater or lesser degree of knowledge of events and appreciation of the issues at stake, backed the central committee. They were, therefore, prime targets for governments that both feared the example of Grenada and had been given the confidence to take pre-emptive moves against those who supported it.

Grenada after the Invasion

Once all opposition had been wiped out, Grenada appeared to be an armed camp and there were fears that it would simply remain a US military base. US troops occupied four of the country's 12 hotels, all public installations, and the Queen's Park cricket pitch in St George's. Point Salines continued to be the centre of their activity. Ambassador Charles Gillespie and his staff were in practice running the country's affairs although, having given himself full executive powers under the declaration of a state of emergency, Scoon was formally in charge.

In response to congressional pressure at home and foreign fears that it was preparing a long-term military occupation — fears that were encouraged by Scoon's repeated requests for the invasion forces to stay for a long period — the Reagan government moved quickly to reduce the size of its garrison. On 3 November 2,500 troops left the island. The same day diplomatic relations with Cuba, Libya and the Soviet bloc were broken and their representatives expelled. With their departure and the clear evidence that there was going to be no further armed resistance 'in the mountains' or elsewhere, the US administration felt sufficiently confident to withdraw all specialist combat troops. Shortly before Christmas 2,000 more soldiers were taken out, leaving a garrison of 300 US troops, 100 of whom belonged to the PSYOPS teams that were directing an all-embracing but far from sophisticated anti-communist campaign in the media. In respect for local feelings the figure of Maurice Bishop himself was not subjected to the vilification heaped upon the Coards and Hudson Austin, but PSYOPS did circulate jokes about Bishop's personal weaknesses and encouraged the view that his political position was one of a foolish idealist.

As US troops were removed, further contingents from the Caribbean took their place although none of the states involved could afford to send large numbers. The question of public order was not, however, as important as that of establishing a new administration that would meet the constantly proclaimed objective of restoring democracy. Governor General Scoon gave every indication of relishing his role as *de facto* executive leader, but he was obliged to relinquish this on 16 November when the state of emergency and curfew were withdrawn. This move was made as a result of pressure from London, the Commonwealth and many of those invited to join an interim administration that would govern Grenada until elections could be called.

The first choice to head this provisional government was Alister McIntyre, a widely respected economist working as deputy secretary of UNCTAD. McIntyre was not in good health, but it was felt that he would not accept Scoon's invitation because although he had been at odds with the PRG, he was on record as opposing the conversion of Grenada into a colony of Washington and approved of a number of reforms undertaken since March 1979. Once McIntyre formally refused the job, PSYOPS began to encourage unflattering comments about him in Grenada. In his place Scoon appointed a personal friend, Nicholas Brathwaite, formerly director of the Commonwealth Youth Programmes Centre in Guyana. Brathwaite was joined by a number of largely undistinguished civil servants who had no attachments with the NJM and proceeded to take very few fresh initiatives other than present requirements for US assistance.

The formation of this new government continued to be troubled when Anthony Rushford, the British lawyer who had drawn up the 1974 constitution and was appointed attorney general by Scoon, resigned within a week. According to Rushford, this was because of the governor general's 'total indifference and lack of co-operation' when he was asked by Rushford, then Grenada's senior legal officer, to provide details of the terms by which he had sought and received US assistance. The attorney general's resignation cast further doubts on Scoon's impartiality and the constitutional basis of the 'request' for a US invasion.

Within days of the landing Washington offered Grenada US$3 million as a grant for 'disaster assistance'. Later it was announced that further aid of US$15 million approved by Congress in December would be disbursed over a number of years. This sum fell far short of the US$30 million calculated by a US team in the country to be necessary for the island's short-term needs, including the completion of the airport. Congress approved only US$110,000 for the improvement of Grenada's very insufficient supplies of water and electricity. At the same time the military set up an office to process claims for damages. By Christmas thousands of requests for compensation had been received but only 250 were approved, at a total cost of US$115,000. All these payments related to destruction caused by US forces when not engaged in combat; Washington refused to accept that it should pay for any damage caused in the fighting whether by its forces or not.

At the time of writing (February 1984) it is too early to state with confidence what the full nature of post-invasion Grenada will be. Although the reduction of US troop levels has somewhat allayed fears that the island would become an offshore garrison, dependence on US economic aid and its political influence may well result in Grenada lacking any authentic independence. Many of the state-based reforms introduced by the NJM are patently at risk and some, such as those concerning literacy and co-operative development, have already been nullified by inactivity rather than edict. A whole series of development projects undertaken in collaboration with non-government organisations and international agencies have been brought to a halt and many people working on them have left the country, either under pressure or because their presence no longer serves any useful purpose. Many community projects have collapsed with the abolition of the national women's and youth organisations. The provisional government is concentrating its energies on strengthening ties with Washington and US capital. As civilian personnel attached to the large new US embassy take over from the military, such ties are likely to become structured and sophisticated. The most obvious expectation is that economic policy will concentrate upon expanding tourism from the US.

Late in January 1984 the White House held an extraordinary press conference simply to announce that Cunard cruises would in future call at Grenada. Cunard president Ralph Bahna emphasised the 'great deal of historical significance' of Grenada and announced that the company's tours would visit places connected with the events of October 1983, such as Maurice Bishop's house, Fort Frederick and Fort Rupert. In a separate initiative, the mayor of Fort Lauderdale, Florida, Robert Dressler, declared that Grenada 'is going to provide a very stable environment for investment' in a 'very pro-American political climate', and announced plans to erect a 250-bed hotel on the site of the prime minister's residence in St. George's. This project would involve an investment of US$2.5 million by private companies from southern Florida and a loan of US$10 million from the US government Overseas Private Investment Corporation (OPIC). At the end of the month OPIC sponsored a visit for 20 businessmen to investigate 12 projects worth a further US$10 million in a country which Secretary of State Schultz referred to as 'a magnificent piece of real estate'.

On the political front Scoon's initial expectations of calling elections within six months have been replaced by a timetable that stipulates a poll a year after the invasion. Public statements to date have indicated that all parties will be able to contest this election. The policy of the NJM remains unclear with the party's scattered leaders issuing different statements. Since the NJM suffered such a severe crisis in October 1983 it is unlikely that it will adopt a coherent and unified policy very quickly. As one Grenadian told *The Times* a week after the invasion, Maurice Bishop would easily have won an election at that time; what remains to be seen is whether the NJM is capable of building upon the memory of Bishop as well as the economic and social reforms of the PRG to retrieve much of the ground it has lost. When the party's traditional enemy Eric Gairy returned to Grenada early in 1984 he was met at Pearls airport by less than 300 people, suggesting that although the eccentric autocrat has lost none of his populist ambitions, the changes introduced after his downfall have deprived him of much support.

Although the crises of October 1983 were without parallel in the modern history of Grenada and had a considerable impact on Caribbean politics, those who have emerged victorious are left with a major challenge. If they are to provide for the genuine welfare of this little island they will have to do much more than simply act according to a constitution, which itself has already proved to be very difficult for them. As time passes the promises and achievements of those who invaded and those who benefited from the invasion will be judged against the limited but real advances made between March 1979 and October 1983. This is especially the case for the younger generation, whose expectations were awakened in a manner that a determinedly pro-US system is not even concerned to match. Although it appears extremely unlikely, it is conceivable that the US will make Grenada a 'showcase' by ploughing in vast quantities of aid, but even if this were done it would not break the legacy of centuries of economic backwardness and would be likely only to reinforce external ties of dependence and an internal imbalance of wealth and power. Confidence that the people of Grenada would, because of the traumas they have recently suffered, readily accept such a state of affairs is, on the basis of past experience, misplaced.

Further Reading

Fitzroy Ambursley, 'Grenada: the New Jewel Revolution' in Fitzroy Ambursley and Robin Cohen (eds.), *Crisis in the Caribbean,* Heinemann 1983.

Fitzroy Ambursley, 'Whither Grenada? An Investigation into the March 13th Revolution One Year After' in Susan Craig (ed.), *Contemporary Caribbean: A Sociological Reader,* Trinidad 1982.

Fitzroy Ambursley and Winston James, 'Maurice Bishop and the New Jewel Revolution in Grenada', *New Left Review,* No.142, Nov.-Dec. 1983.

Caribbean Review, 'Grenada Explodes', Vol.XII, No.4, Miami, Jan. 1984.

S. Clark, *Grenada: a workers' and peasants' government with a revolutionary proletarian leadership,* Pathfinder 1983.

Covert Action Information Bulletin, 'US Invades Grenada — Nicaragua Next?', No.20, Washington, Dec. 1983.

Epica Task Force, *Grenada: The Peaceful Revolution,* Washington 1981.

Epica Task Force, *Death of a Revolution,* Washington 1984.

Forward Ever: Three Years of the Grenadian Revolution. Speeches of Maurice Bishop, Pathfinder 1983.

Grenada is not Alone, St. George's 1982.

Is Freedom We Making, St. George's 1982.

W.R. and B.I. Jacobs, *Grenada: The Route to Revolution,* Havana 1980.

A.J. Payne, *The Politics of the Caribbean Community, 1961-79,* Manchester University Press 1980.

Chris Searle, *Grenada: The Struggle Against Destabilisation,* Writers and Readers 1983.

United States Information Agency, *Grenada: A Preliminary Report,* Washington, Dec. 1983.

Appendices

Appendix One

British Government Policy on Grenada, 1979 to October 1983

The summit meeting of Western leaders on the French Caribbean island of Guadeloupe at the beginning of 1979 could have been a useful showpiece to revive the declining fortunes of James Callaghan's Labour government. However, his absence from Britain during a period of major strikes attracted much criticism, which only grew louder on his decision to fly on from the summit to Barbados for two days of talks with Prime Minister Tom Adams. This apparent disregard for domestic opinion in an election year, uncharacteristic of the pragmatic Callaghan, was mainly prompted by increasing US concern for the future stability of the Caribbean. Callaghan, an avowed atlanticist, had worked hard as both foreign secretary and prime minister to rekindle the Anglo-American 'special relationship', which had cooled somewhat during Edward Heath's drive for membership of the EEC.

The US State Department saw a 'sea of splashing dominoes', in which a single change of regime would resonate through the Caribbean, generating similar revolutions. The British deferred to American fears, and took the initiative in persuading the island governments of the need for a mobile regional defence force with the capability to intervene in any of the participant islands. The main target was the government of Barbados, richest of the small islands and the proposed headquarters for the force.

Reports from correspondents with the Callaghan entourage on Barbados confirmed that security issues were high on the agenda that spoke of Cuban 'expansion' and other external threats. Since Tom Adams had already discussed the regional force idea with St Lucia's leader, John Compton, Callaghan found a receptive audience for his proposal. The two leaders agreed on immediate preparations; a British naval team moved on to the island the following month to supervise the upgrading of the Barbadian coastguard.

In the view of the pro-Western Caribbean Commonwealth leaders, the March 1979 revolution in Grenada made the establishment of a regional security force more imperative. At the time of the revolution Grenadian leader Eric Gairy issued a call from New York for US and British military intervention to restore his position; John Compton and St Vincent's Milton Cato, another hardliner, made similar requests to London. Although the coup appeared to confirm the North Americans' worst fears regarding developments in the region, the record of Gairy's regime was so bad that there was no chance of a positive response from either government. Gairy had become particularly unpopular with the British Labour Party after he had signed a military alliance with Chile. Nevertheless, as a Chatham House paper on the Caribbean pointed out, 'Britain's support for Gairy until the moment of his overthrow is still remembered'.

The immediate security problem for the People's Revolutionary Government (PRG) in Grenada was the threat of a Gairy-backed mercenary invasion. Traditional allies — the US, Britain and Canada — were asked for military assistance. Britain and Canada rejected the request, pledging non-intervention. The US said nothing. The PRG then canvassed Jamaica, Guyana, Cuba and Venezuela, all of whom bar the latter responded. Yet even before this stage the US government had decided on a policy of economic isolation, including the withdrawal of bilateral aid. Grenada's neighbours voted to establish a regional security force 'to counter such future action'. The Labour government, incapacitated by the election campaign, made no further contribution at this point.

The Thatcher government made no immediate statement of policy on Grenada after taking office, but the initial signs were none too hopeful for the PRG. Thatcher declared firm support for US policy in general, and her intention to reduce the level of British overseas aid carried the implication of a more discriminatory distribution policy.

The PRG's forebodings were realized in the first instance by the blocking of export licences for the purchase of armoured cars. An order for two Ferret vehicles was placed by the PRG shortly after the March revolution, for which export licences were granted; but when the order was changed in August to one Ferret and one Saladin, the PRG was told it would have to reapply for export licences. The new applications were rejected at the end of November. An official Whitehall statement maintained that the refusal did 'not reflect on current relations with Grenada but reflects the situation in the area' and made the absurd suggestion that the supply of armoured cars would, in local terms, be the equivalent of 'going nuclear'.

While armoured cars and other military equipment could be procured elsewhere, a reduction in development aid could not be so easily replaced. The £2.25 million grant made at independence was almost totally spent and the PRG made representations to the British government for a new bilateral aid package. The Conservatives had no intention of signing a new agreement and, without saying so directly, made this clear to the Grenadians. Overall aid policy was laid down in February 1980, when overseas development minister Neil Marten told the House of Commons that 'greater weight should be given in the allocation of British aid to political . . . considerations'. At the end of the year, Marten outlined the particular reasons for British displeasure at Grenada:

The present regime has not yet held elections . . . has continued to hold detainees without trial, does not acknowledge freedom of the press and voted in January at the UN in favour of the Soviet occupation of Afghanistan.

Marten's contentions are, to a large extent, spurious: as the Grenadian high commission in London pointed out later in the month, 'it is quite possible to find a number of countries against whom these charges can be levelled . . . (who) continue to receive aid from Britain'. However, the High Commission concluded that,

Grenada is in the process of establishing the kind of society of which the British government disapproves, irrespective of whether the people of Grenada want it or not.

These words were originally spoken by Nicholas Ridley, then a minister of state at the Foreign Office.

Yet British officials continued to deny a halt on bilateral aid to Grenada. In June 1981, the British high commissioner for the Eastern Caribbean, Stanley Arthur, told journalists in Grenada that 'we haven't yet negotiated a new aid agreement with the Grenada government; we haven't said we won't, we just haven't done it'.

Besides aid, the other main instrument of British Caribbean policy was the promotion of the regional coastguard. Thatcher's first foreign secretary, Lord Carrington, arrived in Barbados early in August 1980 at the mid-point of a tour of South and Central America. British assistance for the Barbadian coastguard, initiated by Callaghan, continued under his successor, who implemented the recommendations of the British naval mission to the island. These provided for US$10 million of military aid for the purchase of a 100ft gunboat, the conversion of three shrimp trawlers to armed patrol vessels, and the secondment of British naval officers, including a commander, to the coastguard. The British had also encouraged Barbados in 'going nuclear', providing a grant for the Barbadian army to buy a Sterling armoured car. The vehicle was delivered only weeks after the announcement rejecting export licences for Grenada.

Early doubts from local opposition politicians in Barbados over the wisdom of rearmament were heightened by the operation in December 1979 to recapture the St Vincent dependency of Union Island from dissidents described as 'militant Rastafarians'. The operation also set a precedent in regional security co-operation: while St Vincent's security forces travelled to Union Island, Barbadian troops moved on to the main island to guarantee security. The example was noted both in Barbados, where military development plans proceeded apace, and on other Caribbean islands, who also began to increase their military capabilities. St Vincent, itself backed by a £250,000 grant from the British government, ordered a 25-metre patrol craft from the British manufacturers Vosper Thorneycroft in mid-1980. St Lucia also decided to buy an armed patrol craft. By the time of Carrington's visit, these three islands had agreed on the formation of a joint sub-regional coastguard.

Carrington's agenda included defence and covered additional financial aid to supply equipment for the force's communications hub in Barbados, and the further training of Barbadian personnel. At a press conference after the first

107

day of talks, Carrington reaffirmed that the internal security of the Eastern Caribbean states was the stimulus behind Britain promoting regional security co-operation:

I don't believe that there is an external threat . . . at least at the present time, but I think there are potential threats of subversion of existing governments which the existing governments will obviously wish to fight against. If they ask for our help . . . we shall be very ready to consider it.

A Royal Marine infantry team was later sent to Barbados where it trained personnel from the Barbadian Defence Force and, according to Prime Minister Adams, 'police officers from St Vincent, St Lucia, Antigua and Dominica'. In October 1982, these five states became signatories to a 'Memorandum of Understanding' on security co-operation, in which, 'the parties hereto agree to prepare contingency plans and assist one another on request in . . . threats to national security'.

Carrington was swiftly followed into the Caribbean by Hurricane 'Allen' which wreaked considerable damage in Grenada, St Lucia, St Vincent and Dominica. The banana crop, a mainstay of the regional economy, was particularly badly affected. The four islands co-operate in marketing and research for their banana industries through the Windward Island Banana Association (Winban). At the time, Winban was supported by bilateral aid from Britain under the Windward Island Five-Year Banana Development Programme, worth £4 million in the years 1977-81.

Winban applied to the US Agency for International Development and the British Overseas Development Administration for rehabilitation aid. The British study team assessing the damage omitted Grenada from its itinerary, which St Lucia's foreign minister, George Odlum, described as 'ridiculous' and 'unthinkable'. Both agencies excluded Grenada from the final rehabilitation packages. Objections from Winban were sidestepped by the British and US decision to direct the aid to the local Banana Growers' Associations.

The selective disbursement of aid to Winban members was a potentially counter-productive policy, as the West India Committee, an organisation promoting trade between Britain and the Caribbean, later indicated:

there is strong evidence that the collapse of any one of the Windward Island banana industries could lead to the collapse of the industry in the Windwards as a whole.

The damage to the Grenadian crop was rather less than to those of the other Winban members, and the industry was not in immediate danger of collapse, but Winban feared that the absence of aid-funded items such as fertilizer could impair the quality of the Grenadian crop and hence Winban's whole export operation. In the event, fertilizer and other assistance were secured from the EEC and Canada.

According to Neil Marten, Grenadian receipts from the EEC reduced the necessity for a direct British aid contribution. Nevertheless, other Caribbean countries who benefited from European development funds were also scheduled for aid under a five-year bilateral programme worth £27 million which Carrington announced at the end of his 1980 visit; as the *Financial Times* acknowledged, the Grenadian allocation of £2.2 million scarcely compensated for the total withdrawal of US aid. Britain had not risked isolation in Europe by blocking EEC aid to Grenada but, as the Grenadian high commission in London said, 'it is no secret that Britain's surrogates in the Caribbean have made attempts to discourage the EEC from granting any assistance to Grenada'.

Under the Reagan administration multilateral aid packages became a primary target. Early in 1981 the PRG asked both the EEC and a number of its individual members for financial assistance to build a new international airport, costed at US$70 million. Britain was not approached, having made its position on bilateral aid clear. After intensive US lobbying, five EEC countries withdrew from the negotiations on the grounds that they were already represented by the EEC Commission. The action destroyed the prospect of bilateral aid from Western Europe, although adequate funds were obtained from Cuba, Scandinavia, Nigeria, and Arab sources. The EEC Commission ignored US pressure and awarded £5 million to the project.

The Foreign Office openly agreed with the US 'doubts' as to the character of the airport, but admitted that it had 'no evidence (of) alternative uses' to the declared civil function, which was not surprising since the British electronics group Plessey had won a £6.6 million contract for 'overall project management and the provision of all essential equipment and services' to the airport. The government had underwritten the contract, through its Export Credit Guarantee Department (ECGD), an unexpected decision given the department's stringent policy on Grenada at the time:

Cover is restricted to short-term credit . . . subject to the department's written approval of the buyer. This is necessary because of the continued depressed state of the country's economy and the difficulties of assessing buyer credit-worthiness, particularly in the public sector. Applications for business on longer terms are considered only on national interest grounds.

Since the length of the contract was well over six months' 'national interest grounds' clearly applied in Plessey's case. So, as Plessey later said, 'any question about the nature of the airport would have been totally resolved before the ECGD gave its approval'. The State Department case was further weakened by the award of another airport contract to a US company, Layne Dredging of Florida, for the draining of a lagoon to enable a causeway to be built into the Point Salines complex. Plessey have a close relationship with the British government and are believed to have lobbied hard for the Grenada contract. US objections, if any, could not have been great. Not only was a US contractor also present, trade logic implies that if Plessey did not take the contract some other company would; and if Plessey took it both the British and US governments would know precisely what was being done at the airport. 'We never get out of step with the government when working on a contract', declared a Plessey official.

In April 1983 Maurice Bishop, visiting London, compared Reagan's hostile approach to bilateral relations with that of the British government, which was 'better', although it had been 'very consistent' in its refusal to improve relations. This consistency was exemplified by the outright rejection of recommendations from a House of Commons select committee report examining Central America and the Caribbean. On the matter of aid the

Committee said that,

Grenada still has a strong private sector in its economy and . . . it is in the UK's interest as a trading partner that this should be supported and that Grenada should not be made totally dependent on aid donors who will not support a mixed economy.

The Committee recommended that 'the UK government . . . consult the Government of Grenada with a view to drawing up a new bilateral aid programme'. In reply, the foreign secretary referred to the 1980 aid policy statement from Neil Marten.

The committee also recommended increasing the British diplomatic presence on the island:

we do not believe that the FCO have paid it sufficient attention. The Members of the Committee who visited the island felt that the initial information supplied to them did not reach the usual standards of the FCO.

The government proclaimed itself 'satisfied that the present arrangement is adequate'.

At the time of its publication, several Conservative committee members who had been absent during the compilation of the report publicly disowned it. However, it can be seen from the minutes of the committee's deliberations that the above recommendations were carried unanimously.

The government's dismissive response to the committee's report betrayed a basic lack of interest in its contents, for British policy in the Caribbean is essentially a function of British policy towards Washington. Thatcher is a keen advocate of the 'special relationship', a deformed entity born of Second World War collaboration whose remnants, including complementary intelligence gathering, continue to exert an oblique pressure on British foreign policy. The pursuit of the 'special relationship' leads British governments to fall 'between two stools', in Denis Healey's recent phrase: ineffectual in Washington, out of step in Europe. The practical objective for the British in the 'special relationship' is an ability to influence US foreign policy, the method is to maximise support for American policy. The significance of this for the Caribbean is that there is an ever-growing set of arenas where British and US interests conflict, so that the points of harmony acquire greater importance.

Before Thatcher's arrival at Downing Street, successive British governments had effected a strategic withdrawal to leave only post-colonial anomalies. The residue was a defence commitment to Belize and responsibility for a handful of tiny dependencies. The nature and low volume of UK-Caribbean trade gave little chance for economic clashes between the US and Britain. The absence of many potential causes of friction made Caribbean policy a useful opportunity for the British to embellish their 'special relationship'. British indifference to the Caribbean also assists Anglo-American unanimity. The dearth of British diplomatic representation in the area means that British assessments rely extensively on external sources, particularly those of the US.

Appendix Two

Extracts from the Minutes of the Extraordinary Meeting of the Central Committee of the NJM, 14-16 September 1983

Editor's Note: The meeting lasted for two days and the minutes cover 47 pages of closely-typed text. As a result, there is not enough space here to reproduce the complete report. We are acutely aware of the potential dangers of reprinting only extracts, which may give a false impression of the course of discussion. However, LAB decided that some part of this critical meeting should be presented to the reader, and the editors believe that the extracts reproduced here do at least faithfully represent the tone of the debate as well as indicating the principal issues at stake. We have retained the style and grammar of the original document.

Meeting Started 1.00pm.

COMRADES PRESENT

Maurice Bishop	Phyllis Coard
Selwyn Strachan	Leon Cornwall
George Louison	Kamau McBarnette
Unison Whiteman	Tan Bartholomew
Liam James	Fitzroy Bain
Chalkie Ventour	Chris Deriggs
Ewart Layne	

COMRADES ABSENT

Hudson Austin	(out of country)
Ian St. Bernard	(sick)

. . . Comrade Ewart Layne led off in the discussion . . . The situation is that the revolution now faces the greatest danger since 1979. There is great dispiritiveness and dissatisfaction among the people. Though not in an open way it can be recognized. The state of the party at present is the lowest it has ever been. The international prestige of the party and revolution is compromised e.g. the CC delegates visit to the SU.

We are faced with the tasks of managing the state sector in great economic difficulties, to build the economy in the face of tremendous pressure from imperialism. Politically, to raise the consciousness of the working class and working people in the face of resistance from imperialism and to build the party into a Marxist/Leninist vanguard in a country that is dominantly petit bourgeoise and to carry the proposed constitution to the people in two years' time . . . In the face of all these tasks the party is crumbling, all mass organisations are to the ground, organs of people's democracy is about to collapse. The internal state of the party is very dread. There is wide protest against the higher organs . . . The CC has proven its inability to give

111

leadership to the process . . . The CC is on a path of right opportunism and is very dishonest to its members e.g. in the conclusions of the July plenary it was reported that CC has advanced, every single committee, mass orgs were criticised except the CC and PB (*Editor's note:* Political Bureau) . . . In his view the main problem is the CC. The CC has diverted from the correct path. This will lead to the total disintegration of the party and the collapse of the revolution.

. . . Cde. Ventour supported the points made by Cde. Layne . . . Cde. Leon Cornwall also agreed with the analysis made by Cde. Layne . . . He said that Cuba had similar problems in their development but they were able to develop a militant mass base because of the strength of the party in developing a perspective and its work . . . He also agreed that the CC is on a right opportunist path referring to the conclusions of the July plenary. He continued to say that if the CC is to gain any respect we must move away from this path. He said that this problem is as a result of the low ideological level of the CC and the party in general . . .

. . . Cde. Fitzroy Bain agreed with the position of the Cdes. . . . Party Cdes bramble the masses, a small amount of our firmest supporters are leaving the country. The mood of the party is also lower than the masses at this time . . . Cde. Bartholomew agreed with all the points made so far saying that the CC has not been giving leadership to the process . . . Timidity is a major problem in the party, Cdes are afraid to speak out frankly because when they do they are termed in different ways. Members and CM (*Editor's note:* candidate members) do not understand basic norms of party life. Cdes were not consulted when the three Cdes of the CC was brought on to the PB. Cdes do not know the members of the Central Committee . . .

. . . Cde. Chris De Riggs registering his agreement with the points made referred to the 19 characteristics of petit bourgeois party identified in the weekend of the fedons group seminar highlighting the points on (1) inconsistency (2) insufficient planning (3) vascillation (4) agreement in principle windbagism in practice (5) inadequate vision of the future (6) crisis management (7) poor attitude towards criticism (8) lack of perspective towards future . . .

. . . Cde. McBarnette said that so far this meeting gives a clear indication of how far the CC is from the rest of the membership of the party . . .

. . . Sister Phyllis Coard said that we have to recognize that the situation is very serious . . . The CC has displayed idealism on the question of women in the party, they cannot cope with the demands of the party at this time. She said that she also notice that the older Cdes are getting tired and sick . . . The question of the ideological development of the CC is an issue that we need to make a decision on . . .

. . . Cde. Bishop said that in some ways Cdes contributions have begun to address tomorrow's agenda.

He said that he is struck by the levels of thought and preparation of Cdes as evident in their various contributions though some conclusions are a bit premature, they are however, correct he agreed that the main problem lies in the CC, in his view it have to do with two main factors.

1. Low ideological levels, insufficient knowledge and awareness;

2. The lack of perspective, as evident in a number of CC meetings e.g. 16 July. However, points are coming out more sharply today.

... The CC has made a number of mistakes over the past 18 months because of the weak links with the masses we became bureaucratic and too formalistic in our approach ... His understanding of the criticism and complain from the party has to do with the lack of channels of communications for the membership to raise their complains and grievances which we need to address. He agreed that a lot of criticisms have developed of leading Cdes in the party. He shares the overall concerns that Cdes have arrived at.

Cde. James agreed that there is a serious crisis in the party. There are signs of the beginning of disintegration in the party, drop in confidence and prestige of the CC. If the situation is not rescued there will be no hope for the future of the party and its ability to hold state power.

... Cde. Louison said that ... there is a clear lack of contact with the masses among some of the CC comrades. He feels however, that sufficient weight has not been given to the objective situations and the problems in the economy which we have failed to explain to the masses ... He feels that the CC is still capable of leading, what is missing is the ideological level and collective leadership ... Some Cdes gives a panicky impression in the way they make their points ...

... Cde. Whiteman said ... Too much time is spent on small issues instead of fundamental issues e.g. the Church ... His view is that the leadership must spend more time in house to house in order to know what people are thinking, we also need to think of how to build and sustain the mass organisations in the face of economic difficulties ...

Broad Conclusions Proposed by Cde. Maurice Bishop

1. There is a state of deep crisis in the party and revolution.
2. The main reason for these weaknesses is the functioning of the CC.
3. The crisis has also become a major contributing factor to the crisis in the country and revolution and the low mood of the masses.
4. The crisis has also been compounded by the weakness in the material base, electrical black-outs, bad roads, retrenchments and jobs as an issue.

To correct this situation the following must be done:

1. Find methods of improving the work and individual and collective leadership of the CC.
2. The need to develop a perspective based on ML criterion to guide the work in the coming period.
3. Urgently find creative ways of deepening the links with and out work among the masses.
4. To establish meaningful channels of communications between the leadership and the membership and to formally rationalize the work among party Comrades, bearing in mind the ground swell of complains over work and lack of inner party democracy.
5. The CC need to develop structures for accountability bearing in mind that Cdes are now demanding accounts from the party.

Collective and Individual Analysis of the CC

Cde. Liam James leading off said that this is the last chance for the CC to pull the party out of this crisis and on a firm ML path . . . what is needed is firm Leninism. He pointed out that the most fundamental problem is the quality of leadership of the Central Committee and the party provided by Cde Maurice Bishop. In his view the Cde has great strength, his ability to inspire and develop Cdes, his ability to raise the regional and international respect for the party and revolution; he has the charisma to build the confidence of the people both in and out of the country and to put forward clearly the positions of the party. Today these strengths alone cannot put the party any further in this period. The qualities he lacks is what is needed to push the revolution forward at this time:
1. A Leninist level of organisation and discipline.
2. Great depth in ideological clarity.
3. Brilliance in strategy and tactics.

These qualities which are essential for ML (*Editor's note:* Marxist/Leninist) leadership has proved to be lacking in the Cde. at this time.

Cde. Layne said . . . It is clear that Cde. Bishop lacks these qualities put forward by Cde. James. Despite his strengths, the strengths that he lacks is vitally needed to steer the revolution off the dangers and to come out of the crisis. The salvation of the revolution calls for us to take a mature proletarian decision to save and carry the revolution forward.

Cde. Ventour agreed with the two Cdes that the type of leadership that is necessary to pull us out of the crisis is lacking in the Cde. Leader. These criticisms were made to him on more than one occasion which he accepted. He shows that he do not have the quality to put the party on a firm ML footing.

. . . Cde. Cornwall agreeing with all the Cdes who spoke so far . . . said . . . if we fail to transform the party we will lose state power, lives will be lost, history has placed a great responsibility on our shoulders which we must seek to deal with in the correct and scientific way.

. . . Cde. Bartholomew agreed with what he called very frank and open analysis by the Cdes . . . He agreed with all the points made on the strengths of the Cde. Leader. He continued to say that his weaknesses were known all the while, but Cdes were hesitant to raise them. Though he had accepted earlier criticisms of this, he had never fulfill them in practice.

. . . Cde. Kamau said . . . that the CC continue to be loose and unfocus, he said that the Cde. Leader lacks the quality to lead the CC as spelled out by Cde. James.

. . . Sister Phyllis Coard . . . commented that the main problem of the CC is idealism, volunteerism, failure to face up to hard decisions, illness as a result of psychological pressures in this context. The Cde. Leader has not taken the responsibility, not given the necessary guidance, even in areas where he is directly in charge of the guidance is not adequate. He is disorganised very often, avoid responsibilities for dealing with critical areas of work e.g. study class . . .

. . . Cde. Louison said that the no. one problem is the quality of leadership given the process by Cde. Bishop. He loses focus and spend too much time on details. The points made by Cdes. James and Cornwall have really cristalized the problem which we have to find ways and means of solving. He said, though, that the CC had not been able to assist the Cde. in developing these strengths.

. . . Cde. Leader thanked the Cdes for their frankness in their criticisms. He said that Cdes in the past have given serious thought to the question of leadership and failed to raise it for diplomatic reasons which was not good. He is dissatisfied over the fact that the CC have not raised these points before with him frankly, though a couple non-CC Cdes have done it. He picked up an overwhelming sentiment that the qualities required are not possessed in him. He agreed that the points are correct especially correct application of strategy and tactics which cannot be achieved except the other qualities are fulfil. He had found difficulties in finding a relevant material to study the question of the functioning of the PB and CC which reflects a weakness, he don't think that he had given adequate leadership to bodies. He had several problems over the years especially the style that entails consensus and unity at all costs which can result in blunting class struggle. He had tried to keep a certain kind of relationship with Cdes even though it is not what it used to be before. He also questioned his approach as regards to collective leadership, he said that there is not enough participation and discussions . . .

. . . Cde. James . . . made the following proposals:
. . .
5. Proposed a model of joint leadership, marrying the strengths of Cdes. Bishop and (Bernard) Coard. He went on to define the responsibilities of the two Cdes.

Cde. Maurice Bishop

i. Direct work among the masses, focus on production and propaganda.
ii. Particular attention to the organs of popular democracy, working class, youth masses, visits to urban and rural work places.
iii. Militia mobilisation.
iv. Regional and international work.

Cde. Bernard Coard

i. Party organisation work. Chairman of the OC (*Editor's note:* Organisation Committee).
ii. Party organisational development and formation of Cdes.
iii. Strategy and tactics.

The CC must discuss and ratify all proposals and decisions sought by the Cdes.

. . . Cde. Deriggs commented on the brilliance of the contributions of Cdes Layne, James and Cornwall and supported their position.

. . . Cde. Ventour agreed with the Cde.

. . . Cde. McBarnette agreed with the positions of the Cdes.

. . . Cde. Layne agreed with the position of Cde. James on the question of Cde. Coard's return to the CC and PB.

. . . Cde. Louison said . . . he feels that this model cannot solve the problem of Cde. Maurice Bishop.

. . . Cde. Bain felt that the proposals made by Cde. James is a compromise though it is joining the strengths of the two Cdes. together. He is confused on how this will work.

. . . Cde. Whiteman agreed . . . Cde. Coard should return to the PB and CC, he do not agree with joint leadership, he feels that Cde. Coard should be given specific functions as deputy leader.

. . . Cde. Phyllis Coard . . . agreed with dual leadership not only for a short time but on a long-term basis.

. . . Cde. Liam James for the purpose of Cde. Hudson Austin who attended the meeting on the 16th because of flight problems went on to explain all his reasons for his proposals on joint leadership basically making all the points he had made earlier saying that it we fail to take these measures we will be guilty of right opportunism.

. . . Cde. Bishop . . . said his honest view is that the party must utilise all strengths and talents of Cdes in the party. The greater the strengths of Cdes is the greater responsibility will be given to them. Leadership, power, authority and prestige that goes with leadership goes with rights. He has never had any problem with sharing power, or even a bad attitude to criticisms. He has worked very well with Cde. Bernard over the years from school days, they share a lot of policy decisions, they both wrote the manifesto, the People's Congress endictment of Gairy. He referred to 1977 when Cde. Bernard was accused for aggressiveness and wanting to grab power, he had defended him. His position is that he or anybody has the right to be leader for life, he favours co-operation over competition. He feels that Bernard can come back to the PB because of his skills and intelligence. Cde. James breakdown of responsibility is very useful, however, his concerns is the operationalisation of strategy and tactics . . . He would like to know what is Cde. Bernard's view of the situation and response. If he do not agree what will be the views of the CC. He need to get some answers on the operationalisation. We have to decide how we will articulate this to the party and masses of which a clear position must be drawn up. His personal concerns are: image of the leadership, power struggle, imminent collapse of the revolution.

The formulation of Cdes' criticisms have indicated a clear note of no confidence. He said that they are a two-way flow. He cannot inspire the masses when he have to look over his back or feel that he does not have the full confidence of the Comrades.

. . . Cde. Louison continued to raise his concern in that how will the joint leadership develop the four points in Cde. Bishop.

Cde. James said this proposal will pull us out of the period of crisis and push the party forward along with the full support of the CC and the best efforts of the Cde. Leader will develop these qualities.

Cde. Louison was not satisfied with the answer.

. . . Cde. James: "in the close working together of Cde. Bishop and Coard, the Leader will learn from a working experience." Cde. James brought to the attention of the CC that Cde. Louison is seeking to disturb the proceedings of the meeting for opportunist reasons.

Cde. George also expressed a willingness to leave the meeting.

Cde. James went on to address the point . . . that over the years Cde. Bernard Coard has been able to give guidance to the CC, this does not mean that he will decide strategy and tactics all by himself. However, he will chair all commissions to determine strategies and tactics. The CC will discuss and ratify all proposals brought forward. Also in real life the Cde. has developed strategy and tactics for the party.

Cde. Layne addressing the point on vote of no confidence made by Cde. Bishop said he do not agree with this position. He felt the criticisms were made by all comrades in the spirit of love for the party, ideological clarity and wanting to build a genuine ML party, and to build the working class.

. . . Cde. Louison opposed the fact that he was putting his position for narrow opportunist reasons, he is genuinely seeking clarity on the issue.

Cde. James said that he had spoken of Cde. Louison behaviour and he maintain that position.

. . . Ian Bartholomew said that it took him a lot of guts to make his points. He think that the CC have a very great respect for Cde. Bishop, there is no doubt that the Cde. will remain Prime Minister in the country.

. . . Cde. Louison said that the more the discussions is stretched out at theoretical and tactical levels he becomes more worried . . . On the question of joint leadership he said that he would like to know what is the intention of the CC, if they will like to build the qualities or make a leader through joint leadership and at what stage will the prop be taken off. As an aspiring ML he cannot accept joint leadership, he don't known of any situation of such. He cannot see the dialectics unfold, he is not sure of the evolution of this thing, he cannot see joint leadership helping us.

Cde. Cornwall . . . feels that Cde. Louison is posing the wrong question, as a result will come up with the wrong conclusion.

Cde. Louison said that the joint leadership would not strengthen the revolution. How will it evolve? What will it evolve to? Is it a temporary feature or a permanent feature?

. . . Cde. Layne said . . . the time of manoeuvring is over. The form of leadership is scientifically decided, based on the situation we face . . . The attempt to draw the CC in a personality discussion is a PB (*Editor's note:* petty bourgeois) childish attitude.

Cde. George objected. "He has the right to put forward his position. No one can accuse him of opportunism in his struggle over the years in the party. He raise his points seeking clarity in a genuine way. He regarded Cde. Layne's comments as "shit".

Sister Phyllis Coard said that it is unfair of Cde. Louison to think that there have been demagogy in the meeting. She feels the Cdes have been frank. There has been less demagogy than ever before.

. . . Cde. Bishop . . . expressed his difficulty in chairing the meeting because of the flying of brands etc.

. . . The following positions were voted on . . .

2. Formalisation of Joint Leadership:

For	— 9
Opposed	— 1
Abstain	— 3

Cde. Austin abstained because he was not present for the full discussion for the greater part of the meeting.

. . . Cde. McBarnette proposed that we use a break to ask Cde Coard to come to the meeting for decision to be put to him.

This was seconded by Cdes Cornwall and Layne. Cde. Maurice Bishop opposed it because of the fact that he has to make a personal reflection on the issue. He proposed that the CC meet with Cde. Coard in his absence.

. . . Cde. James had difficulties with the position, he felt that Cde. Bishop should stand up and face the situation because he is part of the Central Committee, he thinks that it can and will affect Cde. Bernard's position on the issue.

Cde. Bishop said that it is difficult for him to understand the question of joint leadership and his own role and function in this model.

. . . Cde. James suggested that the CC meet the following day in the absence of Cde. Maurice to put the decision to Cde. Coard, then work out the package of measures.

. . . It was finally agreed to meet at 1.00pm on Saturday 17th with Cde. Coard.

Appendix Three

Speech given by Fidel Castro in Havana, 14 November 1983

Fellow Countrymen:

On 15 October 1976, a little over seven years ago, we gathered here in this same place to deliver a funeral address for the 57 Cubans who were vilely murdered in the Barbados plane sabotage, carried out by men who had been trained by the US Central Intelligence Agency. Today we have come here again to bid farewell; this time to 24 Cubans who died in Grenada, another island, not very far from Barbados, as a result of US military actions.

Grenada was one of the smallest independent states in the world, both in territory and population. Even though Cuba is a small, underdeveloped country, it was able to help Grenada considerably because our efforts — which were modest in quantity though high in quality — meant a lot for a country less than 400 square kilometres in size, with a population of just over 100,000.

For instance, the value of our contribution to Grenada in the form of materials, designs and labour in building the new airport came to $60 million at international prices: over $500 per inhabitant. It is as if Cuba — with a population of almost 10 million — received a project worth $5 billion as a donation. In addition, there was the co-operation of our doctors, teachers and technicians in diverse specialities plus an annual contribution of Cuban products worth about $3 million. This meant an additional annual contribution of $40 per inhabitant. It is impossible for Cuba to render considerable material assistance to countries with significantly large populations and territories, but we were able to offer great assistance to a country like tiny Grenada.

Many other small Caribbean nations, used to the gross economic and strategic interests of colonialism and imperialism, were amazed by Cuba's generous assistance to that fraternal people. They may have thought that Cuba's selfless action was extraordinary. In the midst of the US government's dirty propaganda some may even have found it difficult to understand. Our people felt such deep friendship for Bishop and Grenada, and our respect for that country and its sovereignty was so irreproachable, that we never dared to express any opinions about what was being done there or how it was being done. In Grenada we followed the same principle we apply to all revolutionary movements and nations: full respect for their policies, criteria and decisions, expressing our views on any matter only when we are asked to do so. Imperialism is incapable of understanding that the secret of our excellent relations with revolutionary countries and movements in the world lies precisely in this respect. The US government looked down on Grenada and hated Bishop. It wanted to destroy Grenada's process and obliterate its example. It had even prepared military plans for invading the island — as Bishop had charged nearly two years ago — but it lacked a pretext.

Socio-economically, Grenada was actually advancing satisfactorily. The people had received many benefits in spite of the hostile policy of the United States, and Grenada's Gross National Product was growing at a good rate in the midst of the world crisis. Bishop was not an extremist. Rather, he was a true revolutionary: conscientious and honest. Far from disagreeing with his intelligent and realistic policy, we fully sympathised with it since it was rigorously adapted to his country's specific conditions and possibilities. Grenada had become a true symbol of independence and progress in the Caribbean. No one could have foreseen the tragedy that was drawing near. Attention was focused on other parts of the world. Unfortunately, the Grenadian revolutionaries themselves unleashed the events that opened the door to imperialist aggression. Hyenas emerged from the revolutionary ranks. Today no one can yet say whether those who used the dagger of divisionism and internal confrontation did so *motu propio* or were inspired and egged on by imperialism.

It is something else that could have been done by the CIA; and if somebody was responsible the CIA could not have done it better. The fact is that allegedly revolutionary arguments were used, invoking the purest principles of Marxism/Leninism and charging Bishop with practising a cult of personality and drawing away from the Leninist norms and methods of leadership. In our view nothing could be more absurd than to attribute such tendencies to Bishop. It was impossible to imagine anyone more noble, modest and unselfish. He could never have been guilty of being authoritarian. If he had any defect, it was his excessive tolerance and trust.

Were those who conspired against him within the Grenadian party, army and security forces by any chance a group of extremists drunk on political theory? Were they simply a group of ambitious, opportunistic individuals, or were they enemy agents who wanted to destroy the Grenadian revolution? History will have the last word, but it would not be the first time that such things occurred in the revolutionary process. In our view, Coard's group objectively destroyed the revolution and opened the door to imperialist aggression, whatever their intentions. The brutal assassination of Bishop and his most loyal, closest comrades is a fact that can never be justified in that or any other revolution. As the October 20 statement by the Cuban party and government put it, 'no crime can be committed in the name of revolution and liberty'.

In spite of his very close and affectionate links with our party's leadership, Bishop never said anything about the internal dissensions that were developing. On the contrary, in his last conversation with us he was self-critical about his work regarding attention to the armed forces and the mass organisations. Nearly all of our party and state leaders spent many friendly, fraternal hours with him on the evening of October 7, before his return trip to Grenada. Coard's group never had such relations nor such intimacy and trust with us. Actually, we did not even know that the group existed. It is to our revolution's credit that, in spite of our profound indignation over Bishop's removal from office and arrest, we refrained from interfering with Grenada's internal affairs even though our construction workers and all other co-operation personnel in Grenada — who did not hesitate to confront the Yankee soldiers with the weapons Bishop himself had given them for their defence in case of attack from abroad — could have been a decisive factor in those internal events. Those weapons were never meant to be used in an internal conflict in Grenada and we would never have allowed them to be so used. We would never have been willing to use them to shed a single drop of Grenadian blood.

On October 12 Bishop was removed from office by the Central Committee, on which the conspirators had gained a majority. On the 13th he was placed under house arrest. On the 19th the people took to the streets and freed Bishop. On the same day Coard's group ordered the army to open fire on the people and Bishop, Whiteman, Jacqueline Creft and other excellent revolutionary leaders were murdered.

As soon as the internal dissensions which came to light on October 12 were manifest the Yankee imperialist decided to invade. The message sent by the leadership of the Cuban party to Coard's group on October 15 has been made public. In it we expressed our deep concern over both the internal and external consequences of the split and appealed to the commonsense, serenity, wisdom and generosity of revolutionaries. This reference to generosity was an appeal not to use violence against Bishop and his followers.

This group of Coard's that seized power in Grenada expressed serious reservations towards Cuba from the very beginning because of our well-known and unquestionable friendship with Bishop. The national and international press have published our strong denunciation of the events of October 19, the day Bishop was murdered.

Our relations with Austin's short-lived government, in which Coard was really in charge, were actually cold and tense so that, at the time of the criminal Yankee aggression, there was no co-ordination whatsoever between the Grenadian army and the Cuban construction workers and other co-operation personnel. The basic points of the messages sent to our embassy in Grenada on October 12 through 25, the day on which the invasion took place, have been made public. Those documents stand in history as irrefutable proof of our clean, principled position regarding Grenada. Imperialism, however, presented the events as the coming to power of a group of hard-line communists, loyal allies of Cuba. Were they really communist? Were they really hardliners? Could they really be loyal allies of Cuba? Or were they, instead, conscious or unconscious tools of Yankee imperalism? Look at the history of the revolutionary movement and you will find more than one connection between imperialism and those that take positions that appear to be on the extreme left. Aren't Pol Pot and Ieng Sary — the ones responsible for the genocide in Kampuchea — the most loyal allies Yankee imperialism has in South-East Asia at present? In Cuba ever since the Grenadian crisis began we have called the Coard group — to give it a name — the 'Pol Pot group'.

Our relations with the leaders of Grenada were to be subjected to profound analysis, as was set forth in the October 20 statement by the party and government of Cuba. In it we also stated that, due to our basic regard for the Grenadian people, we would not rush to, 'take any steps regarding technical and economic co-operation which may jeopardize the basic services and vital economic interest of the people of Grenada'. We could not accept the idea of leaving the Grenadians without doctors or leaving the airport, which was vital to the nation's economy, unfinished. Most certainly, our construction workers wanted to leave Grenada when that project was completed, and the weapons that Bishop had given them were to be returned to the government. It was even possible that our very bad relations with the new government would make it necessary for us to leave much earlier.

The thing that placed Cuba in a morally complex, difficult situation was the announcement that Yankee naval forces were en route for Grenada. Under those circumstances we couldn't possibly leave the country. If the imperialists really intended to attack Grenada it was our duty to stay there. To withdraw at that time would have been dishonourable and could even have triggered aggression in that country then and in Cuba later on. In addition, events unfolded with such incredible speed that if the evacuation had been planned for there would not have been time to carry it out.

In Grenada, however, the government was morally indefensible and, since the party, the government and the army had divorced themselves from the people, it was also impossible to defend the nation militarily because a revolutionary war is only feasible and justifiable when united with the people. We could only fight, therefore, if we were directly attacked. There was no alternative.

It should, nonetheless, be noted that despite these adverse circumstances, a number of Grenadian soldiers died in heroic combat against the invaders. The internal events, however, in no way justified Yankee intervention. Since when has the government of the United States become the arbiter of internal conflicts between revolutionaries in any given country? What right did Reagan have to rend his mantle over the death of Bishop, who he so hated and opposed? What reasons could there be for its brutal violation of the sovereignty of Grenada — a small, independent nation that was a respected and acknowledged member of the international community? It would be the same as if another country believed that it has the right to intervene in the United States because of the repulsive assassination of Martin Luther King or so many other outrages, such as those that have been committed against the black and hispanic minorities, or to intervene because John Kennedy was murdered.

The same may be said of the argument that the lives of 1,000 Americans were in danger. There are many times more US citizens in dozens of other countries in the world. Does this, perchance, imply the right to intervene when internal conflicts arise in those countries? There are tens of thousands of Grenadians in the United States, England and Trinidad. Could tiny Grenada intervene if domestic policy problems arose that pose some threat to its compatriots in any of those countries? Putting aside the fallacy and falseness of such pretexts for invading Grenada, is this really an international norm that can be sustained? A thousand lessons in Marxism could not teach us any better about the dirty, perfidious and aggressive nature of imperialism than the attack unleashed against Grenada at dawn on October 25 and its later development.

In order to justify its invasion of Grenada and its subsequent actions, the US government and its spokesmen told 19 lies. Reagan personally told the first 13.

1. Cuba had to do with the *coup d'état* and the death of Bishop.
2. The American students were in danger of being taken hostage.
3. The main purpose of the invasion was to protect the lives of American citizens.
4. The invasion was a multinational operation undertaken at the request of Mr Scoon and the Eastern Caribbean states.
5. Cuba was planning to invade and occupy Grenada.
6. Grenada was being turned into an important Soviet/Cuban military base.
7. The airport under construction was not civilian but military.
8. The weapons in Grenada would be used to export subversion and terrorism.
9. The Cubans fired first.
10. There were over 1,000 Cubans in Grenada.
11. Most of the Cubans were not construction workers but professional soldiers.
12. The invading forces took care not to destroy civilian property or inflict civilian casualties.
13. The US troops would remain in Grenada for a week.
14. Missile silos were being built in Grenada.
15. The vessel *Vietnam Heroico* was transporting special weapons.
16. Cuba was warned of the invasion.
17. Five hundred Cubans are fighting in the mountains of Grenada.
18. Cuba has issued instructions for reprisals to be taken against US citizens.
19. The journalists were excluded for their own protection.

None of these assertions were proved. None are true and all have been refuted by the facts. This cynical way of lying in order to justify invading a tiny country reminds us of the methods Adolf Hitler used during the years leading up to World War II.

The US students and officials of the medical school located there acknowledge that they were given full guarantees for US citizens and the necessary facilities for those who wanted to leave the country. Moreover, Cuba had informed the US government on October 22 that no foreign citizens, including Cubans, had been disturbed, and it offered to co-operate in solving any difficulty that might arise so that it could be settled without violence or intervention in that country. No US citizen had been disturbed at all prior to the invasion. If anything endangered them it was the war unleashed by the United States.

Cuba's instructions to its personnel not to interfere with any actions to evacuate US citizens in the area of the runway under construction near the university contributed to protecting the US citizens residing in the country. Reagan's reference to the possibility that Grenada might turn into another Iran — a reference calculated to appeal to the US feelings humiliated by that episode — is a demagogic, politicking, dishonest argument.

The assertion that the new airport was a military one — an old lie that the Reagan administration had dwelt on a lot — was categorically refuted by the English capitalist firm that supplied and installed the electrical and technical equipment for that airport. The British technicians of the Plessey company, which has made a name for itself internationally as a specialist in this field, worked alongside the Cuban construction workers, to whose civilian status they attest. Several countries of the European Community that are members of the Atlantic alliance co-operated in one way or another with the airport. How can anyone imagine them helping Cuba to build a military airport in Grenada?

The idea that Grenada was being turned into a Soviet military base is refuted by the proved fact that there wasn't even one Soviet military adviser on the island. The supposedly secret documents that fell into the hands of the United States and were published by the Yankee administration a few days after the invasion refer to the agreement between the governments of Cuba and Grenada by virtue of which our country was to send to Grenada 27 military advisers which could later be increased to 40 — figures that coincide with the ones Cuba published on the numbers of advisers, which was 22 on the day of the attack, to which were added a similar number of translators and service personnel from the mission. Nowhere in those documents that they have been crowing over is there something that has anything to do with the ideas of military bases in Grenada. What they do show is that the weapons that the Soviet Union supplied to the government of Grenada for the army and militia were subject to an article which prohibited their export to third countries. This refutes the idea that Grenada had been turned into an arsenal for supplying weapons to subversive, terrorist organisations, as the present US administration likes to call the revolutionary and national liberation movements. No weapons ever left Grenada for any other country and, therefore, Reagan can never prove that they did.

The assertion that Cuba was about to invade and occupy Grenada is so unrealistic, absurd, crazy and alien to our principles and international policy that it cannot even be taken seriously. . . . The civilian status of the vast majority of the Cuban co-operation personnel in Grenada has been shown to the whole world by the hundreds of foreign journalists who saw them arriving in our country and who were able to interview each and every one of them. Nearly 50 per cent of them were over 40 years old . . . When the US government spokesman asserted that there were from 1,000 to 1,500 Cubans in Grenada at the time of the invasion and that hundreds of them were still fighting in the mountains, Cuba published the exact number of Cuban citizens who were in Grenada on the day of the invasion: 784, including diplomatic personnel with their children and other relatives. The agencies that sent them and the kind of work they did were also reported, as well as the instructions given to them to fight in their work areas and camps if attacked. The fact is, it is inpossible — according to the information we have — for hundreds to remain in the mountains . . . The assertion that the Cubans initiated the acts of hostility is equally false and cynical. The irrefutable truth is that the Cubans were sleeping and their weapons were stored at the time of the air drop on the runway and around the camps. They had not been distributed; there weren't enough to go around and they weren't distributed until the landing was already under way. And that is when the Cuban personnel went to the places assigned to them for that emergency. Even so, our personnel, now organised and armed, had time to see the US paratroopers regrouping on the runway and the first planes landing. That was the invader's weakest moment. If the Cubans had fired first they would have killed or wounded dozens — perhaps hundreds — of US soldiers in those early hours. What is strictly historical and strictly true is that fighting began when the US troops advanced towards the Cubans in a belligerent way. It is also true that when a group of unarmed co-operation personnel was captured they were often used as hostages and forced to lead the way in front of the US troops.

The invasion of Grenada was a treacherous surprise attack with no previous warning at all — just like Pearl Harbour, just like the Nazis. The note from the government of the United States to the government of Cuba on Tuesday 25 October, in an attempted response to our note of Saturday 22 October, was delivered at 8.30 in the morning. Three hours after the landing had taken place and an hour-and-a-half after the US troops began attacking our compatriots in Grenada. Actually, on the afternoon of the 26th the US government sent the government of Cuba a deceitful note that led us to believe that the fighting would cease in a reasonable and honourable manner, thus avoiding greater bloodshed. Although we immediately responded to that note, accepting that possibility, what the US government did was to land the 82nd Airborne Division at dawn on the 26th and attack with all its forces the Cuban position that was still resisting . . . The government of the United States has not condescended to offer the number of people arrested nor the figure of Grenadian losses, including civilian losses. A hospital for the mentally ill was bombed killing dozens of patients. And where is Mr Reagan's promise that US troops would withdraw in a week? . . . Who, then, has told the truth, and who has cynically lied about the events in Grenada? No foreign journalists — not even those from the United States — were allowed to see and report on the event on the spot. The pretext that this prohibition was a security measure for the journalists is both superficial and ridiculous. What they obviously wanted was to monopolize and manipulate the information so they could lie without any let or hindrance to world public opinion . . .

Translated by Prensa Latina.

Appendix Four

US Lawyers' View of the Legality of the US Invasion of Grenada

The following letter appeared in *The Guardian* of 29 November 1983 under the headline 'The way to control Reagan's outlaw leanings'.

Sir, — Throughout the 20th century, the US government has routinely concocted threats to the lives and property of US nationals as pretexts to justify armed interventions into sister American states. The transparency of these pretexts was just as obvious then as it is now. The Reagan Administration has not established that there did in fact exist an immediate threat to the safety of US citizens in Grenada. Nor can the back-up rationale of terminating the 'chaotic conditions' allegedly then present in Grenada be properly invoked to justify the military invasion.

The Organisation of American States (OAS) was the only collective agency mandated by the regional community of states to maintain international peace and security for the Western hemisphere in accordance with the purposes and principles of the United Nations Charter.

Article 18 of the OAS Charter provides that no state or group of states has the right to intervene, directly or indirectly, for any reason whatever, in the internal or external affairs of any other state. Article 20 declares that the territory of a member state is inviolable and therefore may not be the object, even temporarily, of military occupation or other measures of force taken by another state, directly or indirectly, on any grounds.

Finally, article 21 reiterates the solemn obligation of article 2(4) of the UN Charter that American states will not have recourse to force except in cases of self-defence pursuant to existing treaties.

In direct violation of these international obligations the Reagan Administration has forthrightly admitted that it invaded Grenada for the illegitimate purpose of deposing the leftist power after the coup against Maurice Bishop, and then installing a government more favourably disposed to the United States.

The members of the Organization of Eastern Caribbean States (OECS) could not lawfully authorize the US invasion of Grenada. Article 8 of its Charter restricts OECS competence in such matters to situations amounting to an 'external aggression' and then only in accordance with the right of individual or collective self-defence recognized by UN Charter article 51 and in accordance with the OAS Charter.

Furthermore, OECS article 8 requires unanimous agreement among member states before action can be taken, and that condition was never fulfilled here.

If the OECS truly believed the new regime in Grenada created a serious threat to the future peace and stability of the region, the appropriate remedy would have been to bring the matter to the attention of the OAS which possesses sufficient competence to act under circumstances not tantamount to an 'external aggression' or 'armed attack' upon a member state.

For example, during the 1962 Cuban missile crisis the US resorted to the OAS when the Kennedy Administration realised it was not able to justify the 'quarantine' of Cuba under UN Charter article 51 because there existed no immediate threat of attack or aggression by Cuba. Unanimous OAS approval for the quarantine exercised a profound impact upon Khrushchev's decision to remove the missiles.

The Reagan Administration prefers the imposition of unilateral military solutions throughout the Caribbean and Central America.

Both the OAS and UN Charters unequivocally condemn the US invasion of Grenada as a gross violation of the most fundamental principles of international law. Recently 11 members of the UN Security Council and 108 members of the UN General Assembly, among them several staunch US allies, have deplored this invasion for precisely these reasons.

The US Government has suffered the most serious setback to its traditional role in upholding the integrity of the international legal order since President Johnson's strikingly similar invasion of the Dominican Republic in 1965. Even though Johnson subsequently obtained OAS approval this invasion was followed by Leonid Brezhnev's reincarnated version of the Johnson Doctrine to justify the Soviet invasions of Czechoslovakia in 1968 and of Afghanistan in 1979.

In stark contrast to the Johnson Administration, President Reagan has not even bothered to request the OAS to intervene in this matter for the limited purpose of organizing and supervising elections leading to the creation of a democratic government in Grenada, which will raise serious doubts concerning the international legitimacy of any successor government.

US violation of international law sends a strong message to the entire international community that for the US Government the traditional rules of restricting the use of force no longer apply in settling international disputes.

When even the US flouts international law, the only consequence can be an increasing degree of international violence, chaos and anarchy. US military forces are not up to the task of policing the entire globe. And as the War Powers Act proves, the American people would not permit them to do so anyway despite the inclination of the Reagan Administration.

Right now the Reagan Administration seems to be planning an identical fate to Grenada's for Nicaragua under the subterfuge of reviving the moribund Central American Defence Council Pact, which is functionally similar to the OECS's Charter. In order to forestall this the US Congress must enact a Central American equivalent to the Clark Amendment for Angola, which would expressly prohibit the expenditure of any governmental funds in support of overt or covert military or paramilitary operations in the western hemisphere without explicit congressional authorization.

Otherwise the Reagan Administration will continue to provoke a broader war throughout Central America that can serve as a pretext for another round of illegal US military intervention in the region.

Francis A. Boyle, Professor of Law, University of Illinois in Champaign.

Isaak Dore, Associate Professor of Law, St Louis University.

Richard Faulk, Milbank Professor of International Law, Princeton University.

Martin Feinrider, Associate Professor of Law, Nova Law Centre.

C. Clyde Ferguson Jr., Stimson Professor of Law, Harvard Law School.

J. David Fine, Associate Professor of Law, Loyola University in New Orleans.

Keith Nunes, Visiting Professor of Law, Loyola University in New Orleans.

Burns Weston, Murray Professor of Law, University of Iowa.

Appendix Five

Members of the PRG, September 1983

Maurice Bishop	Prime Minister; Minister of Defence, Interior and Carriacou Affairs
Bernard Coard	Deputy Prime Minister; Minister of Finance
Jacqueline Creft	Minister of Women's Affairs; Education
Norris Bain	Minister of Housing
Unison Whiteman	Minister of External Relations; Lands and Forestry
Hudson Austin	Minister of Communications and Labour
Selwyn Strachan	Minister of National Mobilisation
Chris De Riggs	Minister of Health
Lyden Ramdhanny	Minister of Tourism
Kenrick Radix	Minister of Justice
George Louison	Minister of Agriculture
Richard Hart	Attorney General

Appendix Six

Members of the Central Committee of the NJM, September 1983

Hudson Austin (Commander of the PRA; Minister of Communications)
Fitzroy Bain (trade union leader)
Tan Bartholomew (PRA)
Maurice Bishop (Prime Minister; Minister of Defence, Interior, Information, and Carriacou Affairs)

Phyllis Coard (Head of National Woman's Organisation)
Leon Cornwall (PRA; ex-ambassador to Cuba)
Ewart Layne (PRA)
Chris De Riggs (Minister of Health)
Liam James (PRA)
George Louison (Minister of Agriculture)
Kamau McBarnette
Ian St. Bernard (PRA)
Selwyn Strachan (Minister of National Mobilisation)
John 'Chalkie' Ventour
Unison Whiteman (Minister of External Relations)

Appendix Seven

Members of the Revolutionary Military Council, October 1983

General Hudson Austin	Chairman
Lt. Col. Liam James	Vice-Chairman
Lt. Col. Ewart Layne	Vice-Chairman
Major Leon Cornwall	
Major Tan Bartholomew	
Major Ian St Bernard	
Major Chris Stroude	
Major Keith Roberts	
Major Basil Gehagan	
Captain Lester Redhead	
Captain Huey Romain	
Lieutenant Rudolph Ogilvey	
Lieutenant Eman Abdullah	
Lieutenant Kenrick Fraser	
Lieutenant Rayburn Nelson	

Appendix Eight

Leaders of the Countries of the OECS

Antigua-Barbuda	Vere Bird, Prime Minister
Dominica	Eugenia Charles, Prime Minister
Grenada	
Montserrat	David Dale, Governor
St Kitts-Nevis	Kennedy Simmonds, Prime Minister
St. Lucia	John Compton, Prime Minister
St. Vincent	Milton Cato, Prime Minister